BUSINESS COMMUNICATION

BUSINESS COMMUNICATION

Dr. S P MATHUR
MCom, MBA, PhD (Bus. Adm.)
Professor
Department of Management Studies
Sangam University, Bhilwara (Rajasthan)

NEW AGE MANAGEMENT

An Imprint of

NEW AGE INTERNATIONAL (P) LIMITED, PUBLISHERS
LONDON • NEW DELHI • NAIROBI
Bangalore • Chennai • Cochin • Guwahati • Hyderabad • Kolkata • Lucknow • Mumbai
Visit us at **www.newagepublishers.com**

Published by New Age International (P) Ltd., Publishers
First Edition: 2013
Reprint: 2017

GLOBAL OFFICES

- **New Delhi** **NEW AGE INTERNATIONAL (P) LIMITED, PUBLISHERS**
7/30 A, Daryaganj, New Delhi-110002, (INDIA)
Tel.: (011) 23253771, 23253472, **Telefax:** 23267437, 43551305
E-mail: contactus@newagepublishers.com • Visit us at www.newagepublishers.com
- **London** **NEW AGE INTERNATIONAL (UK) LTD.**
27 Old Gloucester Street, London, WC1N 3AX, UK
E-mail: info@newacademicscience.co.uk • Visit us at www.newacademicscience.co.uk
- **Nairobi** **NEW AGE GOLDEN (EAST AFRICA) LTD.**
Ground Floor, Westlands Arcade, Chiromo Road (Next to Naivas Supermarket)
Westlands, Nairobi, KENYA, **Tel.:** 00-254-713848772, 00-254-725700286
E-mail: kenya@newagepublishers.com

BRANCHES

- **Bangalore** 37/10, 8th Cross (Near Hanuman Temple), Azad Nagar, Chamarajpet, Bangalore- 560 018
Tel.: (080) 26756823, **Telefax:** 26756820, **E-mail: bangalore@newagepublishers.com**
- **Chennai** 26, Damodaran Street, T. Nagar, Chennai-600 017, **Tel.:** (044) 24353401
Telefax: 24351463, **E-mail: chennai@newagepublishers.com**
- **Cochin** CC-39/1016, Carrier Station Road, Ernakulam South, Cochin-682 016
Tel.: (0484) 2377303, **Telefax:** 4051304, **E-mail: cochin@newagepublishers.com**
- **Guwahati** Hemsen Complex, Mohd. Shah Road, Paltan Bazar, Near Starline Hotel
Guwahati-781 008, **Tel.:** (0361) 2513881, **Telefax:** 2543669
E-mail: guwahati@newagepublishers.com
- **Hyderabad** 105, 1st Floor, Madhiray Kaveri Tower, 3-2-19, Azam Jahi Road, Near Kumar Theater
Nimboliadda Kachiguda, Hyderabad-500 027, **Tel.:** (040) 24652456, **Telefax:** 24652457
E-mail: hyderabad@newagepublishers.com
- **Kolkata** RDB Chambers (Formerly Lotus Cinema) 106A, 1st Floor, S N Banerjee Road
Kolkata-700 014, **Tel.:** (033) 22273773, **Telefax:** 22275247
E-mail: kolkata@newagepublishers.com
- **Lucknow** 16-A, Jopling Road, Lucknow-226 001, **Tel.:** (0522) 2209578, 4045297, **Telefax:** 2204098
E-mail: lucknow@newagepublishers.com
- **Mumbai** 142C, Victor House, Ground Floor, N.M. Joshi Marg, Lower Parel, Mumbai-400 013
Tel.: (022) 24927869, **Telefax:** 24915415, **E-mail: mumbai@newagepublishers.com**
- **New Delhi** 22, Golden House, Daryaganj, New Delhi-110 002, **Tel.:** (011) 23262368, 23262370
Telefax: 43551305, **E-mail: sales@newagepublishers.com**

ISBN: 978-81-224-3532-0

C-16-10-9690

Printed in India at Ajit Printing Press, Delhi.
Typeset at In-house, Delhi.

NEW AGE INTERNATIONAL (P) LIMITED, PUBLISHERS
7/30 A, Daryaganj, New Delhi-110002
Visit us at **www.newagepublishers.com**
(CIN: U74899DL1966PTC004618)

Foreword

The fast changing environment has made dynamic scenario in the field of communication. The present endeavour in the form of book 'Business Communication' is designed to benefit the students of different streams of communication in the field of Business and Management. The present publication is a proof of author's intensive knowledge and his erudition. It is divided into six major parts and each of them reflects an amalgam of his knowledge and vast experience.

The author has drawn upon his vast experience of learning and teaching from diverse background in writing this book. He has presented concepts, ideologies and performances invariably related to the wide area of communication. More precisely, for the benefits of students, the author has elaborated the study material into different parts and has also included examination-oriented matter.

Having known, Dr. S.P. Mathur for the last over two decades and having read his writing for years, I can only command him for his continued enhanced contribution. I am sure students will benefit enormously from diligent study of this book.

I wish the book and the author all success.

Dr. Anil Mehta
Professor
Department of Business Administration
University of Rajasthan
Jaipur (Rajasthan)

Preface

Over the last few years, innovative and revolutionary changes in the scenario of communication have taken place. Global markets, global trading, differences and increasing customer expectations have led to far reaching impact on communication and transforming of information trends all over the world.

It gives me immense pleasure to bring the first and updated edition of Business Communication to the Graduate, Post Graduate and other professional courses as applicable in different Universities. The basic objectives kept in mind while preparing this book has been to present the subject-matter with entire aspects and to cover the old and new concepts and techniques of communication. The present volume is a modest attempt to incorporate broadly six major areas and in that 17 chapters are distributes. It has been written in an simple language and easy to understand style. Besides conceptual knowledge use of tables, charts and models has been made to make the relevant topics self-explanatory. Besides, at the end of each chapter, the needful short and descriptive type questions are also incorporate.

It is believed that this book will serve a basis for study which will not encroach upon the established subject matter of relevant communication systems.

It is expected that after going through the book the students would get to learn the application of concepts with the various aspects of the subject and develop their analytical ability.

I express my deep sense of gratitude to Dr. Naveen Mathur (Professor - Bus. Adm., University of Rajasthan), Dr. Ved Prakash (Professor, Govt. College, Ajmer) and Dr. Dipin Mathur (Advent) Udaipur for their constant inspiration. I also express my heartiest gratitudes to my wife Asha Mathur and both the daughters for providing needful opportunities, support and encouragement in completion of this work.

I whole heartedly thank to New Age International Publishers, New Delhi which is in the forefront of publications, enthusiastically came foreword to undertake the publication of this unique study.

I firmly believe that the path to improvement is never ending.

—Dr S P Mathur

Preface

Over the last few years innovative and revolutionary changes in the scenario of communication have taken place. Global markets, global trading, differences and increasing customer expectations have led to the revolutionising of communication and the transforming of information trends all over the world.

It gives me immense pleasure to bring the first and updated edition of Business Communication to the Graduate, Post Graduate and other professional courses as applicable in different Universities. The basic objectives kept in mind while preparing this book has been to present the subject matter with [illegible] and to cover the old and new concepts and techniques of communication. The present volume is a modest attempt to incorporate broadly six major areas and in that 17 chapters are distributed. It has been written in an simple language and easy to understand style. Besides conceptual knowledge use of tables, charts and models has been made to make the subject [illegible] self explanatory. Besides, at the end of each chapter, the required short and descriptive type questions are also incorporated.

It is believed that this book will serve the needs of many which will not encroach upon the established subject matter of electronic communication systems.

It is expected that after going through the book the students would get to learn the application of concepts with the various aspects of the subject and develop their analytical ability.

I express my deep sense of gratitude to Dr. Naveen Mathur (Professor, Bus. Adm., University of Rajasthan), Dr. [illegible] (Professor, Govt. College, Ajmer) and Dr. [illegible] Udaipur for their continuous inspiration. I also express my heartiest gratitude to my wife [illegible] and both the daughters for providing me the opportunities, support and encouragement in completion of this work.

I whole heartedly thank to New Age International Publishers, New Delhi which is in the forefront of publications, enthusiastically came forward to undertake the publication of this unique work.

I firmly believe that the path to improvement is never ending.

Dr. S.P. Mathur

List of Tables

List of Models

Contents

Part – VI Barriers and Perspective Effectiveness of Communication

Part - I

Business Communication -General Study

1 Chapter

Business Communication —An Introduction

Communication is a dynamic and decisional process of transmitting the information from one person to the other. It is needful and practical device to make proper behaviour between a 'person' and a 'group'. It is an important and vital part of business and management and contributes some bias and worthwhile aspects for making some interaction among people.

DEFINITIONS

According to **Keith Davis** "Communication is the process of passing information and understanding from one person to another".

According to **Newman and Summer** "Communication is an exchange of facts, ideas, opinions or emotions by two or more persons".

Communication is an important aspect of human behaviour and intentions. It is a decisional part to make some reliable and integrated relations. Communication is more reliable towards determining plans and policies, making sound decisions, co-ordination and to eradicate suspension and proper transmitting the informations.

NATURE AND CHARACTERISTICS OF BUSINESS COMMUNICATION

The features or elements of business communication can be expressed here:

(i) Objectives Task

The contents and messages as included in the framework of business communication are based on some objectives and targets. Different parts of communication are invariably depends on their respective objectives.

(ii) Mutual Approaches

The concept of communication is based on mutual and integrated relations among people and tries to create some approachable contact with each other.

(iii) Multidimensional

The communication is based on multidimensional aspect and thereby it has identified by various structural design like vertical, horizontal and the other. Moreover, it has some variety of activities with its wide ranges.

(iv) Human Process

Basically the process and design of communication are based on not only the efforts but feelings and emotions of human being. The process of communication has invariably depends upon the human ideology and it is needful to develop human aspects in organization.

(v) Arranged and Planned Process

In any concern, the process of communication has, arranged and planned to develop a well defined aspects among those persons who are involved in it.

(vi) A Continues Process

Communication is a continues process and principally it has not got it end. The transmitting of information is going on with both the aspects as forward and backward looking.

(vii) A Mobilize Activity

Communication is the activity to mobilize the human activities, abilities, resources and other things in the society. So, it is a mobilize activity.

(viii) Administrative and Managerial Viewpoints

In any objective based group or organization of communication the systems, techniques, form and processes are more concern with some administrative and managerial viewpoints.

(ix) Bases of Managerial Functions

The concept and approaches of communication are based on determining, implementing the managerial tasks and different technique to achieve some objects etc. in any concern. It is more concern with the level and nature of managerial functions.

(x) Biased for Motivational Aspects

The concept of communication is to motivate the views and feelings of humanbeing towards a particular thing. It is biased to motivate either in positive or any negative form in our society.

(xi) Consensus in Some Sense

It is a foremost feature that it is needful to make consensus by both parties in the same views, consents and with similar sentimental feelings.

(xii) Different Media of Communication

The communication can be expressed its nature, features and different conceptual viewpoints through its various medias like oral, written, audio visual and gestures etc. In fact, the availability, role, utilization and successful factors of communication are being depends upon the role of media.

(xiii) Coordination between Society and Business

Communication is a process in which there is a reciprocal interaction for mutual interest between society and business. It is an important aspect to establish mutual and integrated relations between both of them.

(xiv) Listening Abilities and Capabilities

The effectiveness and successfulness are depend upon the listening abilities and capacities of the concerning partners within communication process.

(xv) Interaction of Human Feelings

Through the communication with transmitting the messages, there have also been transforming the ideas, viewpoints, sentimental ideas and thoughts from one person to the others. It may develop interaction of mutual human feelings.

(xvi) Process by Two Ends

Within the communication process, there are two ends with their destinations. The first and foremost end is the source of message and the second is receiving stage of message.

OBJECTIVE OF BUSINESS COMMUNICATION

In order to conduct various managerial and operational activities of any business organization, there are certain objectives of communication, which are given here as:

(i) To inform the objectives, goals and policies of business organization to their employees as well as other part of the concern;

(ii) To develop and enhance the learning aspects for different partners to perform their task and responsibilities of the concern;

(iii) To provide the training and education to employees and different persons of the concern about their responsibilities and accountabilities;

(iv) To make simple and effective ways of means in the decision making process through different informations, facts and figures;

(v) To develop the motivational aspects through various media and forms of communication so that the level of moral and enthusiasm might be developed;

(vi) To solve some problems and challenges of the concern through effective and reliable role of communication;

(vii) To develop coordination and integration among different major subsidiary activities of the concern.

SIGNIFYING ROLE OF COMMUNICATION IN BUSINESS

In fact, communication has a vital role and it contributes heavily to the success or failure of every human activity along with the introduction of new technologies, expansion of business houses, raising importance of new technologies, expansion of business houses, raising importance of human activity and relations as well as developing new work culture. There have been rising the importance of communication by different aspects as given here:

(i) For Planning

In any organization there is an utmost need and importance of communication in the formation and implementation of planning by effective communication. We can determine and formulate policies, goals, work assignments, standards, methods and strategies through communication.

(ii) Bases of Forecasting

For the success of management, organization and development of different areas of business, the forecasting can accrue an important role. So in order to develop reliable, accurate and worthwhile forecasting there is need to get proper and adequate facts and informations through the process and means of communication.

(iii) Formulation of Organizational Structure

The formation of the organizational structure through the role and impact of different informations is based on the facts and figures as gathered from the means of communication.

(iv) Mutual Cooperation

Through the means of proper communication, there can be developed the cooperation and coordination among different classes of business, by effectiveness and devotion among employees for the concern.

(v) Efficient Operation of Business

The entire operation of business depends upon efficient means of communication. The informations from different functional areas are being important for efficient the operation of business.

(vi) Basis of Managerial Functions

There is an effective and important role of the means and technique of communication for entire functions of management. The aspects of communications can determine and implement the functions of managerial cadres.

(vii) Build up Morale

There is an effective role of communication to build up morale and motivation for employees. Within an effective communication there has been paid proper attention towards, consideration of ideas, views and feelings of them for conducting the work performance. So communication is important for formulation of the level of morale.

(viii) For Formulation of Human Relations

With effective and continues means and technique of communication, there is an efficient possibilities to develop human relations among employees, managers, workers and other persons.

(ix) To Eradic Doubts and Misunderstanding

While creating, developing and utilizing the original facts and informations, there is need to remove doubts and incomplete facts so that several misunderstandings can be eradic properly.

(x) Media of the Contract with External Partners

Presently with the rapid development of informations revolution, there is a great need for managers to make regular and proper contact with external partners. So, that communication would provide some important role to make and develop the worthwhile relations with external partners.

(xi) For Redressal of the Business Problems

There have been possibilities to solve business problems through neutral and effective role of communication and its various aspects.

(xii) Helps in Formation of Goodwill

Through the nature, role and tacts of communication, it might be possible to create and develop the goodwill of the concern. So, there is a need of communication towards forming and developing goodwill.

(xiii) For Effective Control

Every manager tries to get work performance as well as entire role and functions according to predetermined goals, objectives and plans etc. Here there is a great need to check and measure the performing results on the basis of goals and standards. So communication is helpful to make and conduct the control system.

(xiv) For Sound and Prompt Decisions

In order to make rational and reliable decisions there is need to get different informations from various part of business. For it managers are required to get various important facts, figures and informations, so there is a great importance of communication in decision making process.

(xv) For Implementation of Policies, Objectives and Plans

With the help and addicting role of means of techniques of communication and their proper applications, the implementation of policies, objectives and plans can be possible in proper way.

(xvi) For Successful Leadership

It is very essential to transmitting the informations from one person to the other for the successful and effectiveness of leadership. A leader must have the quality of sender and receiver for developing the qualities of leadership.

ELEMENTS OF STEPS OF THE PROCEDURAL FRAMEWORK FOR EFFECTIVE COMMUNICATION

In any business organization it is required to ensure a well defined and identifiable flow of information through interrelated stages or phases towards achieving objective. The major phases or stages within the process of communication can be studied here:

(i) Determine the Objectives of Communication

At the initial stage while starting the process of communication there has been determined goals and objectives. These may be relevant of the managerial and organizational set up of the enterprise.

(ii) Status of Sender

Sender is the person who intends to make contact while passing the message to other persons. This process may be start with the important role of sender, who may be a person, a group, an institution or any other unit. He may also be a superior, a subordinate, a peer or any other.

(iii) Message

Message is subject matter, an important and decisional bias of communication. It is intended to be passed from the sender to receiver. It may be in the form of ideas, opinions, views, feelings, suggestions, orders, facts and figures etc.

(iv) Sources of Message

The preparation of message is invariable depends upon the nature and scope of the sources of subject matter. Sources are also a pivot part while determining the contents and process of communication.

(v) Encoding

It is a transforming process to convert the worthwhile data and informations to the objectives based communication. Since, the subject matter of communication is abstract, so its language, nature, originality, objectively and expressions should be adequately considered in this process.

(vi) Channel Media

In order to develop the transmission of message furthermore, there is a need to determine the nature and availability of channel media. It may develops the relation between sender and receiver as and in the form of written, oral, visual & symbolic etc.

(vii) Overcome the Barrier

Here, it is also essential to find out different obstacles and barriers arising in this process and try to overcome there within the purview of the process.

(viii) Receiver

Receiver is the person to whom the messages as well as symbols are transmitted. He may be a superior, officer, manager, employee or any other person in the organization.

(ix) Decoding

Decoding is the reverse of encoding. The receiver the subject matter of communication and try to express or interpret them according to his objects and requirements.

(x) Feedback/Reaction

It is needful to ensure that the receiver has received the message and understood it according to the senders intended. He may react and change the subject matter for further course of action.

As such, communication has an important part and with the help of different steps, as laid down in procedural framework, it may be possible to make some interactions among different persons.

MODEL NO . 1

Showing the Procedural Framework of Business Communication

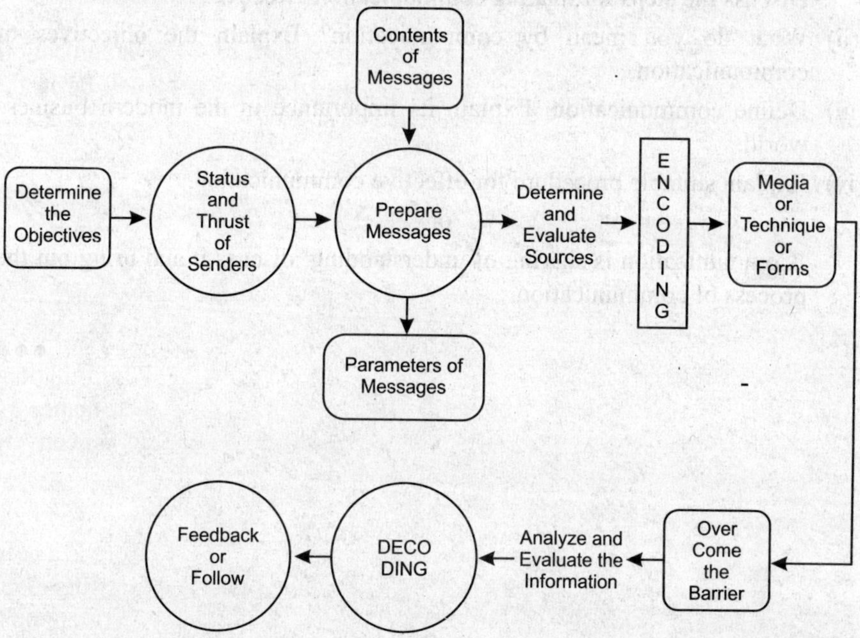

The model depicts the procedural framework for effective communication. It is begin with the determination of objectives. Within the purview of objectives, the sender can determine the required contents, subject matter of the proposed message which depend on the knowledge, skill and command of the senders. Then, the sender prepare the message with the help of predetermined contents and parameters which shows directional way with some limitations. The sources of data and informations may also be evaluated and the means and media of communication might be determined in this process. An important part in this process is to overcome the barriers or obstacles arising out of the situations. Then decoding and verification part can be followed which is based on evaluating and purification of the messages.

As such, in Business and Management the concept and role of communication are being important to develop the perspective behaviour in this direction.

Questions

(a) Short Questions

(i) What is communication?

(ii) Give any two characteristics of communication.

(iii) Give any two objectives of communication.

(iv) Write name of any four importance of communication.

(b) Descriptive Questions

(i) What are the essential characteristics of a good communication system? Discuss the steps for making communication effective.

(ii) What do you mean by communication? Explain the objectives of communication.

(iii) Define communication. Explain its importance in the modern business world.

(iv) Explain suitable procedure for effective communication.

or

'Communication is sharing of understanding' discuss it and bring out the process of communication.

●●●

2 Chapter

Learning Aspects for Effective Communication

Communication is a vital and dynamic part of the organization. It provides interaction and thoughts which aim at making optimum and integrated relations with the persons. The success of every human venture is based on the ability to communicate effectively.

There are different learning aspects to make the contents easy and appropriative. These aspects can provide some language profile like dictionary uses, organizing sentences, vocabulary, punctuation, writing techniques and motivational aspects for making better, fair, reasonable and easy matter in the communication process.

Why to follow learning aspects?

We need to follow different learning aspects which necessitate achieving this skill:

(i) To make language easy and comprehensible.
(ii) To make clear, correct, complete and appropriate subject matter.
(iii) To remove the grammatical mistakes and errors.
(iv) To develop own views, thoughts and concepts of the writer.
(v) To use the punctuation properly for making appropriate and worthwhile content.
(vi) To avoid negative and narrow thoughts and ideas in communication.
(vii) To develop consistency, informality and adequacy in the contents.

DIFFERENT LEARNING ASPECTS

The different learning aspects, for making communication better, are in brief given here:

I. Dictionary Usage

For learning and teaching work expression, the use of dictionary is very important. It is used to learn how to read and it is one of the most often bought books in dynamic way. Dictionaries are printed in almost all languages of the world. It is written almost in language of the world. It is written by language professional to use words and phrases with ease and accuracy.

Objectives of dictionary use

The objectives of dictionary use are as follows:

(i) To manage and develop the usage and meaning of words.

(ii) To manage the phrases, pronounciation and expressing the words.

(iii) To find out the meaning of word and phrases into one language or the other.

(iv) To direct for some special usage of the words.

(v) It develops some devices to use the phrases and words.

Information provided

A dictionary provides some worthwhile information about the words, as given here:

(i) It is helpful to make a process to use the pronunciation of words.

(ii) It provides a system as how a part of speech can be uses.

(iii) It provides significant role to develop the meanings of prefix and suffix.

(iv) It gives the direction as how to break the work with different phrases or into syllables.

(v) It gives special usage of the word.

(vi) It provides a way for some extra and special usage of the words.

II. Vocabulary

Vocabulary is also an important part to use the right word at the right context in appropriately manner. Vocabulary aspects and its process can develop a learning procedure that cannot be stopped.

Learning aspects within vocabulary

Some of the basic learning aspects for vocabulary are given here:

(i) Frequently Confused Words

There are some words which are so similar to each other and create confusion. It is required to make a distinction between them, as their meanings are very different from each other.

Example

Accede – to comply with	exceed – to go beyond
Accept – to take	except – to exclude
Access – admittance, approach	excess – to much
Advise – suggestion	advice – to suggest
Affect – to influence	effect – the result
Allot – to distribute	a lot – much or many
All ready – completely prepared	already – completed earlier

Contd...

Born – given birth to	borne – carried
Capital – money, chief city	capitol – a government building
Cite – to quote	sight – a view, site – a location
Council – a group of people to give advice	counsel – to give advise, a lawyer
Defer – to put off until later	differ – to be different
Device – a mechanism	devise – to plan
Die – to stop living, a tool	dye – to colour
Discreet – careful	discrete – separate
Envelop – to surround	envelop – a cover for a letter
Forth – forward	fourth – number four
Human – of people	humane – kindly
Incidence – frequency	incidents – events
Instance – example	instants – moments
Later – afterward	latter – the second of two
Material – substance	material – equipment in warfare
Miner – mineworker	minor – under-aged person
Moral – virtuous, a lesson	morale – sense of well being
Personal – private	personnel – employees
Principal – sum of money, chief, main	principle – general rule
Rap – to knock	wrap – to cover
Stationary – immovable	stationery – paper
Their – belonging to them	there – at that place
To – a preposition	too – excessively, also
Right – correct	rite – ceremony
Waive – to set aside	wave – araised line of water, a gesture
Weather – atmospheric conditions	whether – if

(ii) Synonyms

Synonyms are single words, which can be substitute for the original word. They have the same meaning as the original word itself. Remember, synonyms are not the meaning of the words. Here, some of the commonly used synonyms. The extensive list may be summarized here:

Anxious – eager	Rebuke – scold
Curriculum – course	Preferred – liked
Formidable – powerful	Distinguished – differentiating

Contd...

Tremendous – enormous	Distinct – clear
Dynamic – active	Incessant – continuous
Inevitable – unavoidable	Consequence – result
Incredible – unbelievable	Panacea – remedyc
Deferred – postponed	Mundane – ordinary
Enumerate – list	Inflexible – rigid

(iii) Antonyms

Antonyms are single words, that are opposite in meaning to the original words. For an exhaustive list, you can use/consult a thesaurus. We can avoid repeated words within a sentence and avoid beginning successive sentence with identical words. A brief list is given below:

Pursue – discontinue	Humble – proud
Decrease – increase	Augment – lessen
Moderate – extreme	Odd – even
Shorten – elongate	Extravagant – economical
Perpetual – transitory	Finite – infinite
Succeed – precede	Obvious – vague
Acquaintance – stranger	Synthesis – analysis
Foreign – native	Informal – formal
Attract – repel	Crisis – stability
Hidden – to show or display	Traitor – supporter
Tact – rudeness	Conspicuous – unknown

(iv) Suffixes

Suffixes are also the parts of a word that are added after a word.

Example:

- ing	- able
- ment	- less
- ly	- ally
- ful	- es
- some	- st.
- er	- ness

III. Organizing Sentence

The forming as well as organizing sentences are also some important aspect to develop learning stream in communication. A sentence is a group of concerning words that express meaningful views and thoughts. It always contains a subject and a predicate also. The objective based subject has some useful message and that must be clear, precise, complete as well as simple for effective communication. It is necessary to learn about sentence construction, to help us to frame appropriate communication. The essential parts for construction of the sentences are as follows:

(i) Subject

It is a part of sentence that can be developed by its objectives and decisional part of the messages. The subject must be clear, complete, and simple within the process of conjunction.

(ii) Verbs

It denotes the work which asserts something or it serves to express some actions. The messages must have to express the verbs.

(iii) Active and Passive Voice

Generally the verb has two voices – active and passive. Both the voices have the same feeling and thoughts. Sentence written in the active voice normally communications more clearly, concisely than that written in passive voice. The passive voice is used when action done is considered than the dues of the action.

(iv) The Predicate

It is a components or a part of sentence that expresses something about the complete sentence. It may be simple, compound or complex sentence.

(v) Use of Tense

There are three tenses like present, past and future. They must be considered while making sentences.

(vi) Phrases

These are the group of related words that contributed to a part of speech. These are used on the basis of verb, noun and objective but they do not contain the subject as a whole.

IV. Summarization

A summary is a shortened version of a matter. It denotes the brief description of a series of event, a task, a process or a play. While summarizing subject matter is writing an essay, an article or a book, we should not include our own views and thoughts on the matter but describe the essay objectively as far as possible. Since the summary eliminates those details that are not needed to include in the subject matter. So in order to avoid repetition of words, duplication in matter, in appropriate prepositions, neglected information and problems of synonyms and antonyms, there is need for making the entire or a long matter in shortened form or summarizing it.

How to write a summary?

Summary is the precise form to make a brief content of any subject matter. For making a summarized form. The steps are given below as:

(i) Try to understand the theme of the matter as well as the title of the subject;

(ii) The entire matter should be gone through time and again;

(iii) The important matter may be underlined and passages may be divided into sections or stages of different thoughts;

(iv) At every stage or point or paragraph, write a sentence in your own language for summarizing the matter;

(v) Check the summary content keeping in view the original passage and matter whatever modifications are necessary for accuracy and completeness;

(vi) Revise the summary matter to ensure its appropriateness;

With the help of summarization, the perfection of communication may be developed to make clear, justified and reasonable words and sentences.

V. Punctuation

Punctuation is also very important in communication or in the use of languages. While speaking or writing, we punctuate our speech or written matter with some appropriate stops. To punctuate means to mark with points, to mark with the usual stops, to put mark of interrogation and the like. Without punctuation marks, it is possible some confusions and misunderstandings may arise. Here, we may need a number of punctuation marks which are commonly used for making communication effective.

(i) Full stop (.)

Full stop or full point to give a period between two sentences;

(ii) Ellipsis (....)

When more than one full point is used, as the basic idea is to leave something unsaid or say something and leave the meaning to be inferred by the other person. It is called Ellipsis;

(iii) The question mark (?)

The question mark may be used at the end of the question. Such questions may be in the form of a word, a phrase or a complete sentence;

(iv) The mark of exclamation (!)

The mark of exclamation is used to indicate a feeling of suddenness, a vehement utterance or an interjection etc.;

(v) Comma (,)

It is a punctuation point which marks the smallest division of a sentence. It shows the smallest interval, break or discontinuity which is deliberately used for effective communication;

(vi) The Semicolon (;)

It is a punctuation mark which makes a division greater than the comma. It is often used when a number of separate or independent clauses are to be separated and a conjunction is not used;

(vii) Apostrophe (')

It is a mark of punctuation showing the omission of a letter or letters in a word. It is basically used to mark the dropping of a letter or a word;

(viii) Quotation Marks (" ") or (' ')

These marks are used to denote the beginning and the end of a quotation. Here, the single words, phrases, sentences or paragraphs may be use. It emphasizes the importance of quoted matter;

(ix) Brackets ([ ])

It is used generally in the printing of enclosed words or any symbols. The words, marks, symbols or phrase may explain a certain contents;

(x) Dash (-)

It shows a break or interval in a sentence or elsewhere. It also denotes a sudden change in thought or any change in the sequence;

(xi) Hyphen (-)

It is a short stroke for joining two words. It is used to separate two words or to show a word which is made up of two or more words. It is used to denote the separate letters and in writing the numerical numbers also.

VI. Writing Techniques

Within the purview of overall communication, we must write as we talk and it is essential to use conversational style at every stage of interaction. Pretend that your reader is sitting opposite to you and you are talking to him or her. Write to express, not to impress.

Basic guidelines for good writing

(i) The contents, subject and verbs always have to be appropriate and agreeable;

(ii) The familiar words are more advisable than unfamiliar ones;

(iii) Don't write run-on sentence and not to use sentence fragments as they are not easy for readers;

(iv) We should avoid mixed metaphors and negative forces because they are the pains in the neck and should be removed;

(v) Try to use proper punctuations wherever required in to the contents;

(vi) To avoid unnecessary and incorrect foreign words, when adequate words and phrases are available;

(vii) Don't use hyperbole unless you are the one person amongst in a million who can use it effectively;

(viii) Don't appreciate unless it is needed;

(ix) Develop positive thoughts and perspective approaches in the language;

(x) There is a need for proof reading carefully to avoid mistakes.

VII. Documentation

It provides some process and system that has to occur and provide future ready references. It provides to collect all evidences or reference material. It shows some written detail or information about some messages or subject. Documents denote some ready reference. Copy of the contents of informative subject. It must be clear, written, specific, within factual manners may or may not be on standardized format and templates.

VIII. Motivational Aspects

Communication is the tool which helps one to achieve the purpose and goal of an organization. It is a needful part to join at the learning process for emerging and developing the role of different words. Here it is needed to make a simple and easy contents of the subject matter. The overall communication system and process are helpful to develop some motivational aspects in the society. For it, the considerable aspects may be summarized here:

(i) To maintain the contents as brief as we can keep to the point and end positively;

(ii) To make a plenty of opportunities to prepare the matter most appropriate and nearby to objectives;

(iii) To make proper interaction between individual and group in an organization on the basis of our subject matter;

(iv) To avoid grammatical mistakes and to use simple and easy language;

(v) It is intended to influence action in order to promote the common welfare of a group or an organization;

(vi) The perspective moving forces are based on suggestive viewpoints which are needed to develop motivation;

(vii) The matter should be persuaded or convince towards better concepts and overall betterment for society at large.

Table 1: Showing the Different Learning Aspects as Applicable for Effective Communication

The different learning aspects, as they are much needful to develop the language command towards making an effective process of communication are as under:

S.No.	Learning Aspects
1	Dictionary Usage
2	Vocabulary
3	Organize Sentence
4	Summarization
5	Punctuation
6	Writing Techniques
7	Documentation
8	Motivational Aspects

Questions

(a) Short Questions

(i) What is meant by learning aspects?

(ii) How to use dictionary?

(iii) What is meant by summarization?

(iv) What are antonym words?

(v) What is the role of vocabulary?

(vi) What is documentation?

(b) Descriptive Questions

(i) Why to study the learning aspects in communication? How to make summarization process effective?

(ii) Describe in detail, the different punctuations in the learning aspect of communication.

(iii) State the writing techniques as may be used in communication.

•••

3 Chapter

Classification of Communication

With the changes in the status, levels and integrated behaviour of the management, there have also been change in the structural design and methods of communication. On the basis of the need, nature, level, transmitting process and mutual relations, there are several forms or types or classifications have been evolved, which are specifically based on the following aspects:

– On the basis of Direction/Flow

– On the basis of Scope/Area

– On the basis of Organizational Structure/Relations

– On the basis of Organizational Status

– On the basis of Media

– On the basis of Nature

OBJECTIVES

The objectives for making different forms/types or classification may be stated here:

(i) The basic objectives of the classification of communication is to perform the directional and instructive functions properly.

(ii) To make clear to the concern about short and long term objectives and targets.

(iii) To make and develop the instant feedback from every part and status of the organizational structure.

(iv) To develop mutual and integrated relations among people of the concern.

(v) To make formal and informal relations among people for better coordination.

(vi) To make strong and stable medias/means for communication.

Communication: Factors affecting the basic Forms/Types/Classification

or

Determinant factors of the basic Forms/Types/Classification

There have been a great change and improve in the level, status, technique and style of communication with the dynamic changes in process and functions as well as interaction between a person and a group. In fact, all the forms types, classifications and sequence of communication are not the similar. But with the technological up-gradation, status of organisational structure are changed and the new horizons have been added there are dynamic modifications in the status of means of communications are emerged. The considerable factors towards determining the types and classification of communication may be stated here:

(1) Nature of Message

The role and effect of the nature of information is an important aspect while selecting proper means of communication. The directions, repetition, dynamism and sequence of messages are included in the nature of informations.

(2) Clearity about Objectives

The objectives of transformation of messages also effect the selection of means of communication. The objectives might be product development, determine market segments, customers' satisfaction, market research and messages about objectives, policies and programme etc.

(3) Coordial Relation between Sender and Receiver

The coordial relations between both the parties have also determine the formation of the means of communication. The friendly and social relations may develop informal and verbal communication in the concern.

(4) Logical Sequence

While the messages involved the logical aspects, the informations may be transformed through some logical means like verbal and gestural and different flow of communications etc.

(5) Positive Approaches

If the sender has the positive attitudes and approaches about the reliability and contents of message, then the sendee may also accommodate himself to adopt it amicably and favourably.

(6) Status of Recipient

Some of the decisional aspects about recipient of the messages like availability, place, status, mental abilities, concepts, behaviour and different other aspects have been duly affect the means of communication.

(7) Secrecy

Sometimes there is need to make secrecy of the facts, figures and different informations. So, the priorities should be given to those means of communication that can be maintained the secrecy for messages.

(8) Understanding of the Process

The functions, procedural as well as technological aspects as laid down in the process of communication have been effect while selecting the means of communication.

(9) Complexities of Problems

In order to solve problems due to the complexities in communication the means of communication might be easy, clear, complete, secret as well as in written.

(10) Clearity of Message

While selecting some means of communication, there is an important factor like clearity and easy expression of the contents of messages.

(11) Past Experience

There is a need to make comparative study and evaluate the past experience concerning means of communication as adopted previously.

(12) Time and Cost Factor

It has to be consider the time and cost factor which have been involved in selecting the means of communication.

DIFFERENT FORMS/TYPES/CLASSIFICATION OF COMMUNICATION

The different types or classifications of communication has to be considered here. The six major classification are described here.

I. On the Basis of Direction/Flows

When communication process has going on with some directional way or when it observe a flow from one point to the other, it is called directional or flow communication. It may classified as given here:

1. Downward Communication

In any organization the downward communication is one that flows from top to the bottom within its authentical structure. When the top or higher level of managerial cadres are transmitted the messages or any information's with the chain of command, it is said to be the downward communication.

It may be in the form of orders, instructions, policies, programmes, directives and praises etc. The objectives or aims of this communication are to provide specific directions, information's and general orders as well as instructions also.

Advantages

The advantages of downward communication are as follows:

(i) It is helpful to express and shows the policies, plans, programmes of the concern organization;

(ii) It provide different needful information, guidelines and directions for performing the job;

(iii) It provides some ideological or value based information to facilitate or encourage indoctrination of goals;
(iv) It helps an executive to apply his authority and powers more effectively;
(v) It helps to coordinate the role and status of hierarchy together;
(vi) It helps in preparing the people to introduce and adopt the change;
(vii) It removes misunderstanding and suspicion.

Disadvantages

The disadvantages of downward communication are given here:

(i) This method tends to promote one way or authoritative communication;
(ii) It is more time consuming as it passes through different levels of organization;
(iii) It is prove to distortions or misuse because it passes through various levels of the organizational hierarchy;
(iv) The information's and messages may be filter or manipulate by some persons for their vested interest. Thus, it can be said that within this communication the messages should be clearly consistent with the rights, duties, responsibilities and capabilities of the receiver. It must be consistent with the policies, programmes and plans of the organization. The messages should also be unambiguous in this system.

2. Upward Communication

In any organization, when communication is transmitted from bottom level to the upper level it is said to be upward communication. In other words, when communication flows from subordinates to superiors along with the chain of command, it is called upward communication.

Advantages

The advantages of upward communication are as follows:

(i) It provides needful feedback for working performance of subordinates;
(ii) It promotes useful ideas and innovative approaches;
(iii) It promotes feeling of belongingness and loyalness among subordinates;
(iv) It may encourage the receptiveness of messages and informations;
(v) It allows subordinates to express their problems and grievances.

Disadvantages

The disadvantages of upward communication are given here:

(i) Subordinates may not provide the entire informations as required by the superiors;
(ii) A lot of distortions have been arising by subordinates;
(iii) There are several problems and obstacles like inaccuracy and incomplete messages have been arising in this method;

(iv) Superior usually do not encourage the subordinate to transmit the information to them;

(v) Subordinates tends to communicate those information which are more favourable for them;

The upward communication may be in the form of progress reports, problems, suggestions, grievances, complaints, appeals and opinions etc.

3. Horizontal or Lateral Communication

When communication takes place between individual or group of some levels or status or positions, it is said to be horizontal communication. When transmitting of messages and informations takes place between some persons of the same level or position of the same department or other departments of the organization. It is also known as horizontal or Lateral communication. It is very applicable whenever the inter-departmental or inter-unit coordination is needful.

Advantages

The advantages of horizontal communication are as follows:

(i) It is helpful in solving the joint problems;

(ii) It ensures quick and proper communication;

(iii) It helps in resolving the inter-departmental conflicts quickly;

(iv) It encourage and develop informal and congenial work environment;

(v) It helps to avoid duplication of work;

(vi) It facilitate inter-unit or inter-departmental coordination.

Disadvantages

The disadvantages of horizontal communication are as follows:

(i) There is a wide chance of misuse and distortion of messages;

(ii) Due to lack of willingness and self interest, this method will not be succeed.

(iii) Due to interrelated conflict, persons are not be able to communicate each other.

Table 2: Distinction between Downward and Upward Communication

There are some differences found in between downward and upward communication. The differences are as under:

S. No.	Basic of Difference	Downward Communication	Upward Communication
1.	Nature	It has an ordering form by nature.	It has suggestive or reporting form by nature.
2.	Media	It is mostly in written as media.	It is mostly oral and verbal as media.

Contd...

3.	Direction of Flow	It is the direction of flow from upper to downward.	It has the direction of flow from lower to upward.
4.	Responsibilities	It is the responsibility of higher authorities to follow it.	It is the responsibility of lower ranks of employees to follow it.
5.	Effects	It is more effective.	It is comparatively less effective.

II. On the Basis of Scope/Area

Scope of communication shows the limitations or boundaries of the area of business in which the communication is performed. On the basis of the scope two broad areas may be studied here:

1. Internal Communication

It is the communication to follow its system and process within an organization. Internal communication is important for imparting a feeling of closeness and cohesion between the employees. It can promote harmony within the organization.

Applicability of Internal Communication

The internal communication can be applicable in various instances as given here:

(i) **Communication with superiors:** Any conversation, reports, or other information that is passed within the company from the juniors to people on senior levels, will be a part of internal communication.

(ii) **Communicating with sub-ordinates:** When managers have to communicate with people who are on levels lower to them, it is called downward communication. It may be in the form of orders, circulars, enquiries, memos and instructions and it can be written or oral.

(iii) **Communication between departments:** In the course of business, all departments have to interact with each other. All the divisions and departments have to keep in touch with each other for proper work coordination.

(iv) **Communicating with colleagues:** It is very important for colleagues to communicate with each other. The more they do it, the more, they will feel past of the entire system. No one can function in isolation. We need to talk to each other to exchange information, which is important in the conduct of business as well as they can build a positive organizational climate that can help the individuals as well as the company.

Advantages

The advantages of internal communication are given here:

(i) The internal coordination among people and different departments can be possible;

(ii) It provide different informations in respect of all the aspects relating to managerial and organization set up;

(iii) It provide some comprehensive informations about the working and process of the organization.

Disadvantages

The disadvantages of internal communication are given here:

(i) It becomes ineffective at the instance of unfavourable situation.

(ii) The incomplete and doubtful messages can create some misunderstanding among people.

The means or measures of internal communications are oral, written, non-verbal and audio-visual systems.

II. External Communication

External communication is communication with external partners or agencies. All the government and private organizations, financial institutions, suppliers, bankers, customers and other environmental agencies that are external to a company, have to communicate with it for various business dealings. External communication that have a long range impact on some specific aspects like product development, investment plans, plant expansion, promotional tasks, community activities and annual reports etc.

Applicability of External Communication

The different aspects to be applicable in external communication are as follows:

(i) The external communication provide a platform for making worthwhile interaction with customers.

(ii) The external communication has provide a proper bias for dealing with the suppliers, marketers and financial institutes as they have decisional and vital role in any business.

(iii) The organizations are required to deal with different legal and statutory aspects through various government agencies.

Advantages

The advantages of external communication are as follows:

(i) It can develop some worthwhile contractual relations with external partners;

(ii) It can create and develop the goodwill of organization;

(iii) The external partners can get the plans, policies and programmes of the organizations.

Disadvantages

The disadvantages of external communication are as follows:

(i) Doubts and differences may be arised due to inadequate and incomplete messages and informations;

(ii) The external barriers may be arised due to some mechanical and defective instruments;

(iii) The language and semantic barriers are also responsible for defective way towards external communication.

III. On the basis of Organizational Structure or Relations

On the basis of organizational structure or relations, the communication may be of two types:

1. Formal Communication

The communication which concerned with formal channel of command or lines for hierarchy of authority is called formal communication.

Some viewpoints emphasized that persons of an organization that work together can construct the communication networks, as per their status and position in the organization. This communication may travel through the formally designed channels. It established the two way communication which links the various positions right from the upward to downward and downward to upwards line of organizations.

Assumptions

The assumptions of formal communication are as given here:

(i) It is communication which is based on some position and authentical status;

(ii) It is interlinked between different posts and positions, not between persons or the group of persons;

(iii) It can be perform on the basis of the rights and duties of the persons;

(iv) There are predetermined arules, processes and functions particularly mentioned in organizational charts;

(v) It may be upward, downward and horizontal communication also.

Advantages

The advantages of formal communication are given here:

(i) The messages are authentical verified;

(ii) All persons may understand their responsibilities and accountability;

(iii) The sequence and continuity may be possible;

(iv) It makes possible to find out the sources of messages and informations;

(v) It helps in maintaining disciplines.

Disadvantages

The disadvantages of formal communication are given here:

(i) There is some delay in the process of communicating messages;

(ii) There are unnecessary and undesirable intervention due to different levels and positions in it.

(iii) It obstructs free, smooth and accurate circulation of communication in an organization;

(iv) It can not develop personal contact and relationship;

(v) The distortion of facts may be possible particularly in upward communication.

2. Informal Communication

Informal communication is concerned with transmitting the messages and informations which takes place on the basis of informal relations among the members of an organization. It is likely a personal communication in practice and not a positional communication. It is not managed or regulated with the formal lines of authority or a formal chain of command. Infact, informal communication arises out of social interaction of people, as **Herbert Simon** has stated that "Informal communication system is built around the social relationship of the members of the organization."

Applicability of Informal Communication

The informal communication sometime referred as 'Grapevine' communication to manage informal relations in the organization. It may be applicable at the two levels as given here:

(a) Individual level

At the individual level, a person can communicate to a person or only one person. They can interact by individual with each or a single person. Some times, this interaction may be called gossip or personal interaction etc.

(b) Group level

At the group level, some persons or a group of persons can interact to other persons or a group of persons, i.e. called group level communication.

Advantages

The advantages of informal communication are as follows:

(i) It is more helpful in making coordial decision making;

(ii) It is more flexible;

(iii) It can develop the motivational aspects within working environment;

(iv) It is more effective and applicable means of communication;

(v) It satisfies the inner urge or needs of the people;

(vi) It is more effective means for communicating the rules, policies, values and tradition of the organization;

(vii) It may provide needful feedback to managerial cadres on their decisions and actions.

Disadvantages

The main disadvantages of informal communication are as given here:

(i) It is difficult to assign the responsibility for handling the informations;

(ii) It may create mislead or misconduct among people;

(iii) It is difficult to believe and trust on informations;

(iv) It leads to leakage of secret informations;

(v) It spread unnecessary rumours and promotes gossips.

IV. On the Basis of Organizational Status

In any organization, there are some status or position as directed by chain of command. The communication on the basis of these status may be divided in two parts.

1. Individual Based

The communication occurs from one person to the other and that are based on the position, status, rights and duties.

Advantages

The advantages of individual based communication are as given here:

(i) The individual communication express the role of a person in organization;

(ii) It can develop the functional relations among different persons.

Disadvantages

The disadvantages of individual communication are given here:

(i) The problems may be arised due to different individual differences;

(ii) Individual emotions and feelings may effect communication process adversely.

2. Group Based

The communication occurs from one person to the group or from one group to the other *i.e.* shows their status specifically of their group status. In other words, when the transmitting of information is perform on the basis of group level due to its role, position and status etc.

Advantages

The advantages of group communication are as follows:

(i) It develop the interaction between individual and group;

(ii) It can develop the integrated & coordinated relations in organization.

Disadvantages

The main disadvantages of group communication are as given here:

(i) With the differences of attitude and vested interest, the communication can not get its proper way;

(ii) When the groups cannot adopt or implement a proper technique or media then it will become very difficult to get proper result.

V. On the Basis of Media

The means and media is also an important type of communication. There are four types of communication on the basis:

(i) Oral Communication
(ii) Written Communication
(iii) Gestural Communication
(iv) Visual Aids Communication

(i) Oral Communication

It is an informal part or media of communication. It shows a process for spoken communication or communication through words or speech.

Characteristics

(i) It is more natural and informal;
(ii) It is a source to make direct relations;
(iii) It is required to the persons as individual and as group to develop their vocabulary constantly involved in it.

Advantages

(i) It is very fast and it save the time;
(ii) It can be more easily kept confidential than written communication;
(iii) It may develop the individual and group identity.

Disadvantages

(i) It provides no record for future references;
(ii) It may not always be possible to save time as there are certain and different circumstances;
(iii) It is not suitable for transmitting lengthy messages.

(ii) Written Communication

It is a media to make an information process which is being used in some writing process.

Characteristics

(i) It has a permanent feature to maintain records for future references;
(ii) It provides reliabilities and worthiness in its message and contents;
(iii) It can build up the images and goodwill of the concern.

Advantages

(i) This media provides permanent and wide evidence;
(ii) It provides an appropriate and accurate contents;
(iii) It has wide coverage; and
(iv) It provide legal evidence.

Disadvantages

(i) It takes time to prepare and complete the transmitting process;

(ii) It is more expensive and costly;

(iii) There is lack of personal touch and emotions.

(iii) Gestural or Non-verbal Communication

It is an interesting and creative part of the overall communication system. In this form, the ideas, feeling and expressions can be possible easily. It may be used for developing a substitute part of oral and written communication.

Characteristics

(i) It is invariably related with the concept of body language;

(ii) It can be consciously created and used with both oral and written communication;

(iii) It can be used as a substitute for words and language also.

Techniques of Non-verbal Communication

(a) Visual symbols

(i) Sign and signals

(ii) Auditory symbols

(iii) Diagrams, graph and charts

(iv) Colours and pictures

(b) Body languages

(i) Facial expression

(ii) Silence

(iii) Personal appearances

(iv) Eye contact and

(v) Smiles

Advantages

(i) It can create and develop some creative and optimistic approaches as well as some innovative ideas;

(ii) It can develop some informal relations.

Disadvantages

(i) This media incurred more expensive at various situations;

(ii) It is difficult to manage and follow some norms for developing the personal appearances.

(iv)Visual Aids Communication

Visuals can be a great way to attract attention through clear message, reinforce the message's impact and raising the dynamic role of speaker. Visual aids can be helpful in supporting text description, explanation of trends, displaying locations and description of relationship among the people. The visual media can be applicable on the basis of its proper and appropriate presentation. The visual media can be stating here:

(i) Pictograms
(ii) Line graphs
(iii) Bar graphs
(iv) Pie charts
(v) Flow charts
(vi) Photographs
(vii) Maps
(viii) Diagrams

VI. On the Basis of Nature

When the communication process or the transactions of messages are not depends upon predetermined objectives and viewpoints but these are invariably related with some specific aspects and due to their dynamic role to be performed in a situation. Moreover, the communication by nature denotes and based on some acceptable views, general behaviour and conduct, specific role and different wide approaches.

The types of communication may be divided into the different parts as given:

(i) Informative Communication

It is basically perform the communication task just only to transmit the message between sender and recipient. There are three main component in it as sender, sendee and media only. In this media, the formal process has not adopting and a simple any available media can be adopted.

(ii) Interpersonal Communication

A transmitting process can be adopted between sender and sendee. It is based on their personal and informal relations and it includes some inner feelings and sentiments of the partners.

(iii) Organizational Communication

The communication process has adopted on the basis of organizational structure. In this media the orders and directions, policies, letters, manuals, complaint books, job description and progress report are being included. All the informations as included in it are more related to the organizational situation, working environment and inter relationship among people etc.

Table 3: Showing the Forms/Types/Classification of Communication

The different forms/types/classification of communication are summarized here:

I	II	III	IV	V	VI
On the basis of Direction/Flow	On the basis of Scope/Area	On the basis of Organizational Structure or Relations	On the basis of Organizational Status	On the basis of Media	On the basis of Nature
1. Downward	1. Internal	1. Formal	1. Individual Based	1. Oral	1. Informative
2. Upward	2. External	2. Informal	2. Group Based	2. Written	2. Inter Personal
3. Horizontal				3. Gestural	3. Organizational
				4. Visual Aids	

Questions

(a) Short Questions

(i) Define Downward communication.

(ii) Define Informal communication.

(iii) Describe any two advantages of Written communication.

(iv) What are the types of communication on the basis of Non-Verbal communication?

(v) What are the advantages of External communication?

(vi) What is 'Gestural' communication?

(vii) What is Interpersonal communication?

(b) Descriptive Questions

(i) What is meant by 'Communication'? Describe the classification of communication on the basis of organizational structure or relations.

(ii) Describe the advantages and disadvantages of the classification of communication on the basis of scope or area.

(iii) Describe the advantages and disadvantages of the classification of communication on the basis of media.

Part - II

Media/Types of Business Communication

4 Chapter

Oral Communication

Oral communication occurs in speaking and listening that we use at several instances. It shows a process for spoken communication or communication through words or speech. This communication is more natural to speak when the other person is present. It may be more effective when there is some informal situation among different persons at that time.

CHARACTERISTICS OF ORAL COMMUNICATION

The characteristics of oral communication are given here:

1. Oral communication is more natural;
2. It develop the immediate effectiveness among the partners;
3. It is a source to make informal contact and relations;
4. It requires that both parties should be present and attentive at the same time;
5. It may develop some communication bias for formal and informal interactions;
6. It requires that the persons as individual and as group to develop their contentment involve in it;
7. It shows some personal success and achievements of an individual;
8. In respect to get record of the message, the oral message may be taped for later references;
9. In order to prepare the message appropriate, justified and shorter, it is needful to prepare some preliminary and closing remark in the message;
10. The cost of this communication depends upon the size and time of message transmission more over the presence of partners is also an important aspect in determining cost factors;
11. It develops and allows immediate feed back. There is continuous exchange of ideas and views. The speaker can modify and clarify the message on the spot.

Advantages

Oral communication offers the following advantages:

(i) Oral communication is very fast and it saves the time involved in it;

(ii) It build upon an effective and personal touch among the different partners;

(iii) Oral message can be more easily kept confidential than written message;

(iv) It satisfies one of our deepest need in any human organization to establish individual and group identity;

(v) It may be helpful to develop informal relations among different persons in any organization;

(vi) It save the money spent on supporting material and stationary in an organization;

(vii) It provides an opportunity for developing fast and immediate feedback among the people;

(viii) It provides an opportunity to the speaker to correct himself and can modify his voice, speech and tone etc.

Disadvantages

The disadvantages of oral communication can be summarized here:

(i) There is poor retention, as the listener cannot retain oral message in his memory for a long time, while the speaker himself may not recall what he actually said;

(ii) The dumbest comments, wrong messages as well as using unsocial words may create the negative feelings of listens;

(iii) It provides no record for future reference and as such it has not legal validity;

(iv) Sometime it may not always be time saving as there are certain and different circumstances in the society;

(v) Sometimes it is likely to be confused and misunderstood due to unclear message, partial message, poor vocal expressions and noise and inattentiveness of the partners;

(vi) It is not suitable for transmitting lengthy messages;

(vii) In most of the cases people take less care, when speaking process have developed than the writing process;

(viii) If there is a long distance between speaker and listener, then there may arise some obstacles in it;

(ix) If these have been some unhealthy or bad relations between speaker and listener, then there will be certain obstacles or problems may arise.

Channels of Oral Communication

There are certain methods or techniques for oral communication. These techniques have been useful for both the parties for channelising the message from one person to the others. These techniques or channel are stated here:

1. **Eye contact**

   The eye contact among some persons or from one person to the others is also a part of oral communication. This contact can develop or add some signifying status of transmitting the words. It is a part of face to face presence and expressions of partners.

2. **Face to face conversation**

   The face to face conversation is the best and practical aspect in oral communication. It denotes the personal identification & develop immediate and direct flow of communication and makes close presence of the living personality.

3. **Presentation**

   A presentation is a well-prepared talk, written presentation or a speech to known and unknown persons. Mostly, a presentation is always followed by the questions from the audience.

4. **Tone of the voice**

   The oral message can get a technical status through a tone of the voice which occurs by sender. The tone of voice like pleasant, unpleasant, fast speed, pitch variation, volumes and pause etc. develop the channel of oral message.

5. **Body language**

   This communication can be supported and developed by the speaker's body language. Generally, the body movements of a person are guided by his thoughts, feelings and behaviour. The different movements of part of our body like head, eye, face, gestures body shape and postures can provide some oral communication to the others.

6. **Gestures and postures**

   Gestures and postures refers to the movement of our arms, legs and hands which can develop a positive or a negative impressions among the other persons.

7. **Interview**

   An interview is a formal or informal meeting in which a person or a group of persons discuss a matter with another person. It is characterized by question and answer type of oral communication.

8. **Public speech**

   A public speech is given to a large audience. Basically it has a face to face conversation and it aims to develop transmission of message from speaker to listeners or audience.

9. Group discussion

It is a formal or an informal meeting constitutes of about eight to ten persons for discussing a given topic. It is very stimulating and better platform for channelising the oral message to other partners.

10. Meetings

Meetings also have a part of the channels of oral communication. A meeting usually involves many persons and it is directed or guided by a person, who has the leading capacity to manage the communication process properly.

HOW TO MAKE ORAL COMMUNICATION EFFECTIVE

The precautions as given here may be taken to make oral communication more effective.

1. The speaker should use his natural way of speech. He may cultivate a pleasing voice, easy words with some natural styles.
2. A good speaker must understand the listener before talking. He should put himself in place of the listener, prepare and adjust his message according to the needs, abilities and situations of listeners.
3. The speaker should not use irrelevant, baseless things and messages. Here, he must evaluate, find out the situation and requirements of the audience.
4. The speaker should pronoun his words clearly and correctly. He tries to speak distinctly, properly and slowly. The clarity of expression must be the basic aim of oral conversation.
5. The speaker should monitor his speed of speaking. It is so important to learn and imbibe the appropriate speed of dialogue delivery.
6. The message should not overload and it must avoid the appearance of abrupt and discourteous. Moreover, it should not be vague or incomplete in all respect.
7. There is a need to prepare a logical sequence of different ideas, viewpoints and information as being involved in a message. The part or components of the message should be arranged in a logical order.
8. To provide some chance or to allow your listeners to clear their doubts as well as to solve the quirees etc.

Listening as a Tool of Communication

In order to develop proper oral communication, the listening is an important part. Oral communication can not be effective without proper listening. Listening requires much more attention as more or less it is a deliberative efforts. The important points for developing a worthwhile listening process may be stated here:

(i) To appreciate the speakers' message and informations;

(ii) It required that listeners must ask the questions and seek clarification wherever is necessary;

(iii) The listeners' might emphatically be able to feel the emotions and feelings of the speakers;

(iv) The listeners must appreciate the views, outlooks and concepts as give by speakers;

(v) The speakers must use the feedback mechanism to check the appropriateness of matter;

(vi) Try to create a positive listening environment.

Questions

(a) Short Questions

(i) Define oral communication.

(ii) Describe any two characteristics of oral communication.

(iii) Describe any two advantages of oral communication.

(iv) Describe any two methods/channels of oral communication.

(v) Describe any four basic guidelines for making effective oral communication.

(vi) How does listening may be improved?

(b) Descriptive Questions

(i) Define oral communication and also describe its characteristics.

(ii) Describe advantages and disadvantages of oral communication.

(iii) What is meant by oral communication? Also state suitable measures for effective oral communication.

●●●

5 Chapter

Written Communication

Within the channel and means of communications, the written communication has an important and decisional part. When the means or media of transferring the message in 'writings' that is called written communication. It is a media to make an information process which is being used in some writing process. Everything that is put down on paper by writing comes under the purview of written communication. Generally, it includes letters, circulars, notices, forms, memos, manuals and reports etc.

CHARACTERISTICS OF WRITTEN COMMUNICATION

The written communication have different attributes and some of them are given here:

(i) Written communication requires much more time than oral communication;
(ii) It has a permanent feature to maintain records for future references;
(iii) It provides reliabilities and acceptability's in its message and contents;
(iv) The efficient and reliable presentation is more or less depends upon the acceptability and intentions of readers of the written message;
(v) Written communication can build up the image and goodwill of the concern;
(vi) It shows the views, outlooks, thoughts and ideas of the writers.

CHANNEL OF WRITTEN COMMUNICATION

Written communication has a wide area and it is used for many purposes. The methods or means of written communication are being discussed here:

1. Letters

Letters are the most widely and comprehensive used form and means of written communication. They are commonly used particularly for external communication. A letter has an objective based layout which has to be carefully prepared as each part of the layout is needed for reference. Overall subject matter of a letter has not only given some message, but it shows the credit or goodwill of the concern. It may be sent by mail, courier, fax and e-mail etc.

2. **Memo**

   Memo is usually an informal message between members of the same organization and generally relates to daily work. It is used to convey information and instructions with brief messages. There are normally used the pads of memo and pre printed formatted papers for exchange of short messages. A memo may or may not be signed and it can be personalized for top executives.

3. **Notice**

   A notice is used when many people have to be given the same information in the organization. It is the most popular and common method for mass communication within an organization. A notice can put on notice boards to develop a wide range of interaction.

4. **Circular**

   A circular is a detailed document giving informations, instructions, guidelines or orders on a specific matter. It has a date for reference, proper title and is signed by the authorized person. Circular are generally issued by official bodies and head of the organizations. They are sent by mail or fax or e-mail or with persons also.

5. **Report**

   A report is a detailed document prepared by an individual or a committee entrusted with the task of collecting information on a given subject. It requires careful research, collection of data and presentation of the findings, conclusions and recommendations. Reports are of varying length and may be in a wide size as per its matter involved in it.

6. **Minutes**

   Minutes are the written record of decisions taken at a meeting. Different bodies have their own convention of recording the discussion and the decisions. Minutes may be written by hand or typed and pasted in a minute book or types and filed in a minute file. Minutes are a legal document.

Advantages

The advantages of written communication are given here:

1. **Permanent evidence**

   A written matter or documents are permanent to large extent and can be used in the future for reference.

2. **Accurate and appropriate**

   The written matter usually formulated with great care as it can be checked any time. So the matter has the quality of its accurateness and appropriateness.

3. **Wide coverage**

   It is only the means of communication in which the sender and receiver of the message are separated by long distances. As such, written messages and contents have widest possible coverage.

4. **More transcribed**

   Written matter can easily be reproduce or make a new copy of transcription for a new shape in ordinary way.

5. **Identical actions**

   Some time there is uniformity in order and procedures and other message that can develop some identical actions etc.

6. **Repeatedly referred**

   A written message is convenient as it can be taken up for further corrections. Any partner, including the writer of the document can view it repeatedly for any needful reasons.

7. **Legal evidence**

   Written message may be used as legal evidence and it is more reliable and acceptable as documentary proof.

8. **Lengthy message**

   Written communication is very suitable for involving some detail matters and transmitting lengthy messages.

Disadvantages

Written communications suffers from following drawbacks:

1. **Lack of secrecy**

   Sometimes it is difficult to keep and maintain the written message secret.

2. **Time consuming**

   It takes time to prepare and complete the process as involved in written communication. As much time is wasted, it is not suitable when it is to be sent immediately.

3. **Costly**

   Written communication is more expensive than oral communication. All the supporting materials and the process of writing message are very costly.

4. **Feedback is slow**

   In this communication the immediate feedback is not possible. Both the time and means as taken in it consumed a lot of time.

5. **Rigidity**

   Written communication lacks flexibility on the spot and immediate clarifications and modifications in written message can not be made.

6. **Impersonal**

   Generally the written messages used to be formal and there is lack of personal touch.

Thus, the written communication is an important and dynamic part in the process of information transmitting work. It enables to create and develop the communication task properly in the organization.

BASIC PRINCIPLES OF WRITTEN COMMUNICATION

The basic principles of some worthwhile guidelines for making a better and effective written communication are given here:

(i) The written message must be reliable and authentic,

(ii) The contents must be appropriate and situation based,

(iii) The contents must be able to make a documentary proofs as well as for future references,

(iv) The message must be in perspective and develop the suggestive aspects within the communication scenario,

(v) The message must be clear and cover all the needful aspects of the content,

(vi) The message must develop the credit and cooperative behaviour of the writer,

(vii) The message must develop and prepare its contents for effective manner towards transmitting in computer network.

(viii) The writer must follow as much as the guidelines for grammer & language formation.

QUESTIONS

(a) Short Questions

(i) What do you mean by 'Written Communication'?

(ii) Write any two characteristics of Written Communication.

(iii) Define 'Memo' and 'Notices' in Written Communication.

(iv) Describe in brief the advantages of Written Communication.

(v) How does the Written Communication could be effective?

(b) Descriptive Questions

(i) Define Written Communication. Also state the advantages and disadvantages of written communication.

(ii) Describe different methods/channels of Written Communication.

(iii) What are the basic principles or guidelines for making Written Communication effective?

●●●

6 Chapter

Non-verbal Communication

Non-verbal communication is an interesting and creative part of the overall communication systems. It may be used for developing a substitute part of oral and written communication. Within this part, the ideas, feelings and expressions can be managed as well as sharing our experiences can be possible easily. At the early stage of origin of human life, the people communicated with another by using some sign language or gestures through their body parts. It is more correlated with body languages. As such, the communication through symbols is called non-verbal communication.

CHARACTERISTICS OF NON-VERBAL COMMUNICATION

The different aspects of communication which more or less related with oral and written communication can be improve or get some effective role, might be included in non-verbal communication. The basic elements or characteristics of non-verbal communication are as follows:

(i) Non-verbal techniques can be used as a substitute for words as well as language also;

(ii) It is mostly involuntary and unconscious and almost it is not perfectly controled.

(iii) Non-verbal methods helps to make mutual coordination between oral and written communication;

(iv) It is invariably related with the concept of body language;

(v) This communication can be consciously created and used with both oral and written communications;

(vi) Basically it is effected and develop a better situation on the basis of the ideas, concepts, inner feeling and outlooks of the concerning persons;

APPLICABILITY OF NON-VERBAL COMMUNICATION

Non-verbal communication has been based on proper coordination between some part of oral and written communication. Within the part and process of over all communication, the non-verbal aspects have some independent position but it may be applicable in different areas such as:

(i) It is more applicable in trade and business areas particularly in advertising field;

(ii) It is applicable when it is needful to express some emotions and inner feelings of people;

(iii) It is more applicable when to convey the information to illiterate people for example, the warnings for smoking and traffic signals can easily be applicable for different people.

(iv) It is more applicable for conveying facts and informations through maps, charts and graphs etc.

(v) It is more related with those situations wherever the vocal and sound related methods are used.

METHODS/TECHNIQUES/AREAS OF NON-VERBAL COMMUNICATION

The different methods/techniques or some area of non-verbal communication can broadly be divided into two parts:

I. Visual Symbols

Through the visual symbols a sender can manage and present in a compact form and be able to express some relevant and suitable information in right direction. Within the purview of non-verbal communication the different symbols are as given here:

(i) Diagrams, graphs and charts

Diagrams are simple presentation of facts and some illustration towards operating few problems. Graph and charts also an important part to represent some facts and statistical informations. At a glance the graphs may be presented in vertical and horizontal form as well as the charts can be made in many ways *i.e.* bar charts and multiple charts. Every graph and chart must be based on some relevant scale or key to explain the information and symbols etc. They must also have proper title and labels to show what information it represent.

(ii) Colours and pictures

Colours are an important and effective means of communication colours can develop and influence the status of mind of the people. They represent pleasure and regret situation in the society. It is also used to distinguish different products and their brands etc. Pictures can also be used to express some words or messages. Generally pictures are used in advertising, photography, brochures and posters etc. These may be used in a wide area and attract the feelings, viewpoints and thoughts of people.

(iii) Sign and signals

A sign is a mark used to represent or express some message or information; - Skill and cross bones for danger', + for plus, X for multifications. A signal is a command or directions which indicate some warn precaution and guide lines for achieving some predetermined task. Both of the signs may be used by a group or an individual may be made with some lights, maps, diagrams and drums that can be seen or heard at a distance.

(iv) Auditory symbols

Auditory symbols provide some needful warns and direction to the people at various situations. It denotes some authentically as well as compulsion conveys the message from one side to the other. In this way, sound is used in major cases. For example **Sirens** to warn about enemy air raids, warn of fire or accident. **Bells** are used to indicate the starting and ending of work periods. **Beeps** are used by most electronic gadgets.

II. Body Language

Within the process of communication, human body and its various parts play an important role. The study and analysis of messages conveyed by body movements is known as body language. It denotes some changes that occur in the body position and movements that reflect what the person is feeling or thinking. The identification of body movements can make some results or some new things as given here:

(i) It appears to convey some messages;

(ii) It shows some feelings and thoughts etc.;

(iii) It express some emotions of a person;

(iv) It dominate some interaction among people;

(v) It reflects the biological, mental, habitual, social and cultural attitudes of a person.

DIFFERENT ASPECTS OF BODY LANGUAGE

Body language consists of many aspects which are given here:

(i) Personal appearances

An individual's appearance can shows or help to establish his or her identity as well as recognition in society. In fact, to a great extent, we are what we appear to be. A personal appearance depends on several things like physical appearance, hygiene, individual's features, grooming, clothing accessories and style etc. All these aspects can change or modify the appearance of an individual. Appearance develop some messages as in the form of impression.

(ii) Eye contact

The eyes of persons are especially very expressive and communicate our deepest feelings. Eye contact is of great importance in face to face communication. Eyes shows concentration, surprise, fear, happiness and influence of other.

(iii) Facial expression

The face is an important and powerful means of non-verbal communications. It develops primary site for expression of emotions. A cheerful face or a gloomy face influences to a great extent. The facial expressions can convey some messages or informations through feelings and reaction of an individual.

(iv) Smiles

The smiles are also an integrated part of the entire role of body actions. It express a joyful feeling with some positive acceptances. It is a part of facial expressions.

(v) Gestures

Gestures refers to the movements of our hands, arms and legs etc. Waving our hands signifies a greeting and represent some words. Some of the body movements such as leaning forward, slouching, fidgeting or walking briskly all fall into this category.

(vi) Silence

The silence is also an important part within transmitting some messages to different people. It is very emotionally powerful way to convey a variety of responses. It create and shows satisfaction, anger, love, resentment, importance and lack of interest etc. which can convey some messages to others.

(vii) Touch

If demonstrate the physical touching among different persons. It may be at the individual and group level also. Touching with a part of the body shows some affection and it may express some message to other person.

Table 4: Showing the Methods/Techniques/Areas of Non-verbal Communication

The different methods/techniques or some area of non-verbal communication can broadly be divided into two parts:

I. Visual Symbols	II. Body Language
(i) Diagrams, Graphs and charts	(i) Personal Appearance
(ii) Colours and Pictures	(ii) Eye Contact
(iii) Signs and Signals;	(iii) Facial Expressions
(iv) Auditory Symbols	(iv) Smiles
	(v) Gestures
	(vi) Silence
	(vii) Touch

ADVANTAGES OF NON-VERBAL COMMUNICATIONS

The advantages or merits as arising from non-verbal communication are given here:

(i) It can create and develop some creative and optimistic viewpoints and approaches at the working place;

(ii) It can develop some informal interaction among different persons in an organization;

(iii) It is especially important in exchanging feelings and emotions among people;

(iv) It can develop some innovative ideas and thought at the right direction.

DISADVANTAGES OF NON-VERBAL COMMUNICATION

(i) The means and techniques of non-verbal communication incurred more expensive at various situations;

(ii) It is difficult to manage and follow some norms for developing the personal appearances;

As such, the non-verbal communication is very useful means to express the feelings and emotions by which some sort of communication can be developed.

QUESTIONS

(a) Short Questions

(i) What is meant by Non-Verbal Communication?

(ii) Describe any two characteristics of Non-Verbal Communication.

(iii) Describe any two means of Non-Verbal Communication.

(iv) What is meant by 'Visual Symbols' in non-verbal communication?

(v) What is meant by 'Personal Appearances' and 'Eye contact'?

(b) Descriptive Questions

(i) What is meant by non-verbal communication? Describe the advantages and disadvantages of Non-Verbal Communication.

(ii) Define non-verbal communication. Also state different methods or techniques of non-verbal communication.

(iii) What is 'body language'? Explain its methods or techniques as applicable in business communication.

●●●

Part - III

Commercial and Employment Communication

7 Chapter

Business and Commercial Communication

In a dynamic of commercial scenario, the correspondence has an important and decisional aspect to develop mutual interaction among different people and organization. The commercial structure as well as its network at any place or in any environment includes the trade, business, industry and different services.

The correspondence in any field of business/commerce is a process of passing information and proper understanding from one person to the others. Communication is an important and decisional part not to develop the business correspondence but also to make a promotional platform in it.

OBJECTIVES OF BUSINESS/COMMERCIAL CORRESPONDENCE

(i) To make the exchange of ideas and informations from one person to the others;

(ii) To make a dynamic process in changing environment for growing and developing the commercial activities;

(iii) To provide assistances towards making proper interactions among persons involved in commercial sectors;

(iv) To interpret and understand the facts, figures, informations and statements related to commerce and business etc.

(v) To provide mutually needful informations to different business units.

NEED AND IMPORTANCE OF BUSINESS/COMMERCIAL CORRESPONDENCE

Today, in business scenario, the role and different aspects of correspondence have a decisional part and develop a large scale of operations. These correspondences are related with the letters and other written communication at large. The need and importance of commercial correspondence are given here:

(i) For making a business contact with different customers;

(ii) For asking or confirming about the supply of raw material and other infrastructural facilities to different business units;

(iii) For making contact with different local Government and non Government bodies and concerns;

(iv) It is beneficial to outcome or promote the product and services in market;

(v) It is helpful to solve the customers' grievances and complaints;

(vi) For making a settlement of accounts at different stages of business cycle;

(vii) For making some worthwhile contact and business relations with debtors and creditors;

(viii) For making the employees development programmes;

(ix) For conducting 'day to day correspondence with different commercial parties;

(x) For managing and organizing the import and export trades.

BUSINESS/COMMERCIAL LETTERS

Business/Commercial letters are important part within the field of its correspondence scenario. It is a media to make proper and formal interaction among all the partners who are involved directly or indirectly in business transactions. It may be in the forms and types of different classification on the basis of their objectives and nature etc.

MAIN COMPONENTS OF THE LAYOUT OF BUSINESS LETTER

The main parts of business letter are as follows:

1. **Heading or Letter Head**

   A letter is usually a first visual contact with another person or organization. In any business letter, we must have notices the top part of the paper. It usually consists of a printed part which contains the name and a complete mailing address and telephone numbers of the concern. The personalized or executive letter heads are also used that is also an important part to visualize the initial introduction for the concern. The letter heads occupies an important place so it is essential to know the requirements of a professional and attractive letter heads. It is needful to consider that the title or letter head part should not occupy more than one fifth of the paper space. There should not or words i.e. B.S. instead of 'Bhilwara Spinners'. The email and fax number should be written with all needful information. The relevant STD/ISD code number must also be mentioned at all appropriate places. As such, the letter head must be neat, clean and represent the concern as a whole.

2. **Date Lines**

   Every business letter must be dated in all respect. Here, the date and month is spelled out in full, with in cne line and the year is written in all four figures. This enables quick reference in the future and to prepare filing easier.

3. **References**

   The references denotes the letter number, file number, subject code or number and other filing details to make it easy to locate the file related to the issue. Some concern used both as 'Our reference number' and 'Your reference number'. It was already printed on the letter and it was treated as outdated practice.

Table 5: Showing the Major Components of the Layout of Business Letters

The layout of the commercial correspondence specially of letters is an important part. The major components of the layout of business letters are given here:

Main Points of Layout	Sub-parts and Beneficial Points
1. Heading or Letter head	(i) Shown the name of address of sender; (ii) Display the identification of letter writer.
2. Date line	(i) Date and months must be spelled out in full; (ii) Quick and future reference.
3. References	(i) Easy to locate file numbers; (ii) R code numbers;
4. Inside address	(i) Display the name and address of the receiver; (ii) Neat and clean appearances.
5. Special marking	(i) It gives nature and importance of the letter; (ii) It shows main thrust of the letter.
6. Subject line	(i) For proper clarification; (ii) For referring the target and subject.
7. Salutation	(i) It use stylist way with honorable feelings; (ii) Addressed to the receiver.
8. Body of the letter	(i) Main contents and matter of the letter; (ii) It displays the relevant details.
9. Complimentary close	(i) It develop a relative aspects; (ii) It may analyze the subject.
10. Signature	(i) Shows the name and designation of sender.
11. Enclosures	(i) It shows the supporting documents for the letter.

4. Inside Address

Inside address is also an important part of any business letter. It consists of the name and address of the receiver as it appears on the front and main part of letter. The words that appears honour to a person like Mr., Shri, Mrs. Or the designated words must be used here. The inside address may be typed in block form and the address should be clear and neat in all respect.

5. Special Marking

It provide some special attention to the receiver or reader of the letter. If a letter is confidential, it is indicated above the inside address either at the margin or in the centre. It may be used by the words 'confidential', 'urgent', 'important' and 'attention' etc. It may be either in all capital or with initial capital and underlines.

6. Subject Line

It gives a brief description for making a reference of the subject of the letter. It aims to make the clarity of the letter, especially if the letter is complicate and have a longer period of time. It is placed either above or nearby the salutation place. Generally it is used by the word subject.

7. Salutation

Salutation part develop the stream of mutual relations. This part locate at the space below the inside address. It is followed by some stylish way and it has no punctuation mark. The salutation matches the first line of address. If the letter is addressed to an organization, the salutation is plural: Gentlemen or Dear Sirs or Sir. If the letter is addressed to a particular official mentioned only by designation e.g. 'The Production Manager'. If the official is a lady the salutation is Madam or Dear Madam.

8. Body of the Letter

This is the main part of the letter that contains the message or the information to be communicated. Generally all the letters are types with single or double space with same paragraphs. Within these lines, after salutations and before end of the complimentary part, the main body is full of information which should display some new and positive approaches. The main paragraph should contain all the relevant details. It contain the crux of the letter. The purpose and intention as well as the needful matter should be involved in it without any omissions. As such the main body may be consisted of the main parts as

(i) The opening and targeted paragraph;

(ii) The main paragraph and

(iii) The closing paragraph etc.

9. Complimentary Close

The complimentary close or line is written with one line or the two below the last line of the text matter. It is placed on the right and is followed by comma. While written the complimentary close, the first word should begin with a capital letter, for example 'Yours faithfully', 'Yours truly', 'Truly Yours' and 'Yours truly' etc.

10. Signature

Signature may disclose the name and identification part of the senders of the letter. It is placed just below the complimentary close. It is very useful that the writer is giving assent to whenever has been mentioned in the letter. The signature is usually hand written. It can be facsimiled if too many of the same letters are being sent. The senders' identification may appear on the line below the name. If a letterhead has been used, the letter may end with the name and designation. But if the letter has been written on plain paper, the company's name may be typed two lines below the complimentary close in capital letters.

11. Enclosures

Enclosures are related documents which have to be sent along with the letter. The enclosures are placed behind the letter and clipped or stapled along with it. If there is more than one enclosures, they are numbered and placed in the order of their serial numbers.

The enclosures may be indicated in the business letter at the ending part of left side with the words – Enclosures', Encl., 'Encls' or the name and title of the enclosures.

PATTERNS OR STYLES OF THE LAYOUT OF COMMERCIAL LETTERS

Layout denotes the framework or design in which the different parts of the letter are placed. It may arrange the order to all the parts viz. headline, date line, subject line, main body of the letter, salutations and the other components. Some of the styles can be descried as given here:

I. Full Block Form

This is the most modern style of layout of business letters. There is no indentation at all, but every line including date line, complimentary clause and subject line begins at the left margin. The address has no punctuation at the end of the line. Though it has a wide scope but some companies do not like this form because it looks heavy on the left and rather blank on the right. The date and signature parts can not be seen unless the letter is fully shown or open after taking it in files.

Examples

14th May 2011

Saraswati Coaching Institute
12, Greenways Road,
Gurgaon

Sir,

We offer extensive coaching classes to the students of B.A. and B.Com. classes. Our teachers are qualified. We also provide them computer training and competitive knowledge. Our fees are very affordable.

We invite you to send your children to join our institute.

Yours faithfully

Proprietor

II. Modified Block Form

It has a slight modification of full block form. It is stated that date line and complimentary clauses are on the right side as their usual position. The salutation and complimentary clauses are followed by comma. All the paragraphs begin at the left margin. The inside address may be mentioned in block form. It appears neat and readable particularly in the filling process. It can be referred to easily by the date, even after it has been filed.

Examples

14th May 2011

Saraswati Coaching Institute
12, Greenways Road,
Gurgaon

Sir,

We offer extensive coaching classes to the students of B.A. and B.Com. classes. Our teachers are qualified. We also provide them computer training and competitive examinations. Our fees are very affordable.

We invite you to send your children to join our institute.

Yours faithfully

Proprietor

III. Hanging Indented Form

The letters for commercial purposes are based on hanging indented form is used as sales letters. The inside address is in block form. The date line and complimentary clauses are on the right side. Each paragraph start on the left margin. At every stage of lining, the every further lines of each paragraph are intended 3 to 5 spaces from the left margin.

This is used for publicity and products campaign through some brochures. The opening line of every paragraph 'HANGS OUT'. Here the main paragraph are highlighted with some striking words like BEWARE, CAUTION, RUSH IMMEDIATELY. Some words like 'On', 'The' are not used in it.

IV. Noma Form

It is known as American style of letter writing. It has been adopted by National Office Management Association of America. It is usually adopting by some prominent business houses. In this form all the lines begin at the left margin. It has no salutation but the inside address is in the block form. There is no need to mentioned the complimentary clause. The writer's name and title are typed in capital letter, one line below the space for signature. The typist's initial are also included in the left bottom corner.

Example

Saraswati Coaching Institute
12, Greenways Road,
Gurgaon

INFORMATION ABOUT OUR INSTITUTION

We offer extensive coaching classes to the students of B.A. and B.Com. cources. Our teachers are qualified. We also provide them computer training and competitive examinations. Our fees are very affordable.

We invite you to send your children to join our institute.

Yours faithfully

Proprietor

FORMS/TYPES OF COMMERCIAL CORRESPONDENCE

There are several forms or types available to make correspondence for commercial purposes. Here the name of some of the forms or types of commercial correspondence are given here:

1. Letter for buying orders;
2. Letter for reference;
3. Letter for credit transaction;

4. Advertising copies and mass media;
5. Credit and status enquiries;
6. Letters to debtors;
7. Letters to creditors;
8. Meeting notices and agenda;
9. Minutes of meeting;
10. Annual reports of a company;
11. Circular letters;
12. Price quotations;
13. Letter for complaints and claims;
14. Sales letters;
15. Collection letters;
16. Bank correspondence;
17. Correspondence with different institutions or organization;
18. Business letters to Government authorities;
19. Letters for import and export;
20. Microsoft and internet etc.;
21. Memo;
22. D.O. letters.

Above all correspondence with letters are more or less related to the business or commercial communications. Their layout and structure are duly based on the components as provides some directional way within the previous pages. In respect of the informational documents as adopted in company organization a separate chapter is being presented for it.

Questions

(a) Short Questions

(i) Define the Commercial Correspondence.

(ii) Define the 'special marking' in business letters.

(iii) Write short notes on:

- Window cover.
- Complimentary clause.
- Noma forms.

(b) Descriptive Questions

(i) What are different forms/types of Business letter?

(ii) What is meant by commercial correspondence? What are the objectives of Commercial Correspondence?

(iii) What are the different technological appliances used for Commercial Correspondence?

●●●

8 Chapter

Office Communication System

A business organization or concern performs several functional activities with the help of several communicative assistances of their office. The office in any organization has the central part to organize and perform day to day tasks. It is the place that represent the organization and provide various facilities to internal and external part of concern through different means and systems of communication. Communication is an important and decisional part to provide different assistances for performing the business tasks properly. Here, there are several methods and systems that have included in this study.

OBJECTIVE OF OFFICE COMMUNICATION SYSTEM

There are certain methods and devices through them the informations can collect and provide to different part of the business or the concern. The objectives of information system are given here:

(i) To collect different data according to the need and requirements of the concern;

(ii) To maintain the records of the data and various informations through different methods of filing and computer systems;

(iii) To develop the information processing and transforming among different functional areas of business;

(iv) To manage and organize different office tasks such as letter formation, typing, data storage, data analysis, filing, answering phones and reply of received letters etc.

NEEDS AND IMPORTANCE OF OFFICE COMMUNICATION

There are great importance of the office communication system in the concern. The importance are given here:

(i) It provide adequate and appropriate informations to different persons;

(ii) It provide faster response in savings the time for further processing of data and informations;

(iii) It provide an effective platform by which the principles and functions of management can be implemented;

(iv) It provide the facts, informations and different noticeable messages by which effective coordination can be implemented;

(v) It provide some needful techniques and systems by which the creditable goodwill can be developed in the corporate sector and market also;

(vi) It enables to develop wide processing from centralized area to desktop computing for proper networking;

(vii) It enables to develop some opportunities for more friendly interfaces with end-users;

(viii) It develops greater involvement of end-users in I.T. implementation.

METHODS/SYSTEMS OF OFFICE COMMUNICATION

In any concern there are several methods and systems of office communication. With the emergence of office automation, the systems are incorporate by the technological advancement. Here, in order to make proper study the methods may be classified on the basis of old methods as well as of new and technological methods. Both the methods shows some gradual phases of the technological developments in the field of business communication.

I. Old and Traditional Methods

In office communication the old and traditional methods are given here as:

(i) Orders

Orders are important part to provide various informations, facts and notices which are being transferred from top level of management to the lower level of employees. It enables workers and employees to know about policies, programmes, required work performance, job contents for better results.

(ii) Circulars

Circulars are also a traditional document to prepare the general and common matter to inform different persons or department in the concern.

(iii) Office note

It is prepared by the office staff which shows some intention and basic norms to implement some programme with the help of employees. It is being feasible with authorized or permitted by the manager or some senior persons.

(iv) Notice

It is displayed at the common place to notify some specific or general informations and other contents of communication. It is a general and most common method to interact with mass people.

(v) Reference letters

These letters are more concerned to provide some references of some prominent persons, units or some branded products in business areas. Mostly, the credit and payment transactions depend on them.

(vi) Reports and manuals

In any concern the employees can intimate about their work performance and results to the top officials through their reports. In manual the persons can determine proper work assignment, rights and duties and organizational structure etc.

(vii) Advertisement

According to **Wheeler**–'Advertising is any form of paid non personal presentation of ideas, goods or services for the purposes of inducing people to buy.' The management and conduction of advertising process is the part of any office in any concern, so it is directly and indirectly concern with the office information system.

II. New and Automation Systems

With the advent of technological innovations, the office work has perform through office automation. It is technically based on computer system which includes new hardwares and software packages with combination of different support systems. The roles of MIS and servers have been contributing a lot in the processes of office automation that makes office employees more productive. The combinations of information technologies that have a dramatic impact on day to day office operations are called office information system. The new methods are given here.

(i) Desk Top Publishing (DTP)

It is computer based document to prepare printed document. It is driven and monitor by DTP software. Here, the high quality based screen enables us to display on screen looks exactly like the hardcopy that will be created by the laser printer. DTP applications can be developed different reports, correspondences, news letters, manuals, slides, advertisements, brochures and other documents etc.

(ii) Computer Aided Design (CAD)

These refers to computer systems that develop some new specifications for display screen interface to data base the design of various products. It is widely used in engineering areas.

(iii) Electronic Bulletin Boards

In it the different partners and customers can transmit their data and informations to the other group for collecting the needful records. Basically, it collect and provide the information about customers' profile. It may increase responsiveness to product and market forces and significant improvement in the process of customers' services.

(iv) Facsimile

Some of the general technologies like telephones, modems and scanners, graphics are being used in it for transforming the data and informations.

(v) Internet

The internet is a global network of millions of computers that are interlinked by various channels of communication.

(vi) Voice Mail

It is a simple method based on oral communication, within it, the sender dictates a message by speaking them over the telephone rather than typing them. The message is transmitted into a digital messages through a special device called a codec.

(vii) Electronic Mail (E-mail)

It is a system that allows a person or a group of person to communicate electronically with others in written through a network. It has a wide range and popular form of business communication.

(viii) Archival Storage

It is the basic function in the storage process of computer. The archival data is placed onto various media and stored them at off line. The most common technologies are magnetic taps, optical disks, diskettes and output microfilms etc. These processes can develop some documentation of data and informations.

(ix) Multimedia

It is the combination of different group of computer technologies that integrates different types of media such as text, graphics, animation, audio and video to generate informations.

(x) Video Conferencing

Within computer network two or more persons at different sites can transmit audio-video data for conducting a conference which is called the video conferencing. Each person has a video camera, microphones and speakers mounted on his computer. As the two persons speak to one another, their voices are carried over the network and delivered to the other speakers and whatever images appear in front of the video camera appears in a window on the other person's monitor.

(xi) Fax

It is sometime called telecopying, that is the telephonic transmission of scanned printed material (both text and images), normally to a telephone number connected to a printer or other output device. The original matter is scanned with a fax machine, which processes the contents i.e. text or images etc.

(xii) Online Chat Tools

Wikipedia describes chat tools best: "Online chat can refer to any kind of communication over the internet, but is primarily meant to refer to direct one-on-one chat or text-based group chat using tools such as instant messengers." It is commonly used in place of e-mail when there is a need to communicate live. Chat tools can be used both for internal and external communication and can be placed on a website so that customers can talk to a customer service person in real-time. Utilizing chat tools usually requires a free software download system.

(xiii) Client Server Computing

It is an approach and device to network use by means of a desktop computer. Here, the server is an important part that provides a control function for the network servers store and process data to users across the enterprise and these data can then be accesses by client system for different processing requirement. It is based on communication services, system analysis and desktop computing programmes.

Table 6: Showing the Methods/Systems of Office Communication

The different old and traditional as well as new and automation system as listed here:

I. Old and Traditional Methods	II. New and Automation Systems
(i) Orders	(i) Desk Top Publishing (DTP)
(ii) Circulars	(ii) Computer Aided Design (CAD)
(iii) Office note	(iii) Electronic Bulletin Boards
(iv) Notice	(iv) Facsimile
(v) Reference letters	(v) Internet
(vi) Reports and manuals	(vi) Voice Mail
(vii) Advertisement	(vii) Electronic Mail (E-mail)
	(viii) Archival Storage
	(ix) Multimedia
	(x) Video Conferencing
	(xi) Fax
	(xii) Online Chat Tools
	(xiii) Client Server Computing

Questions

(a) Short Questions

(i) What is meant by Multimedia?

(ii) Define Teleconferencing.

(iii) Define Desk Top Publishing.

(iv) Define Electronic Mail.

(v) What is Client Server System?

(vi) Define Video Conferencing.

(b) Descriptive Questions

(i) What is meant by office communication system? Explain the need and importance of different types of system.

(ii) What are the objectives of office communication system? Explain the old and traditional systems of office communication.

(iii) Describe the different new and automation office communication systems.

●●●

9 Chapter

Communication in Company Management

Company may be described to mean a voluntary association of persons who have come together for carrying on some business and sharing the profits therefrom. According to **Prof. Haney** - "A company is an artificial person created by law, having separate entity, with a perpetual succession and common seal."

The Companies Act, 1956 the law in our country in this regard is a consolidated and worthwhile piece of legislation.

In corporate environment, several complications and hindrances are arising out of the provisions and policies as described in the legislations and act. So in order to remove & solve the complications, the phenomenon of communication might be able to make proper interaction with the relevant persons & follow the legislations etc.

IMPORTANT DOCUMENTS OF COMPANY ORGANIZATION — BASIS FOR COMMUNICATION

Here, the different documents as needful to manage the company's organization, might not be only helpful to implement the legislative provisions, but also to overcome the complications and communication barriers. The major documents are as listed here:

1. Memorandum of Association
2. Articles of Association
3. Prospectus
4. Annual Accounts and Audits
5. Registers and Returns
6. Notice of Meetings
7. Agenda
8. Minutes
9. Resolutions etc.

1. Memorandum of Association

Memorandum of Association of a company as originally framed or altered from time to time in pursuance of any provision of law or act. "It is a document of great importance and it contains the objects for which the company is formed and therefore identifies the possible scope of its operations beyond which its action cannot go.

This is the primary document of the company and it is sometimes called the charter or constitution of the company.

Contents

The memorandum contains informations in respect of the aspects as given here:

(i) Name of the company
(ii) Place and address of the company
(iii) Objects of the company
(iv) Capital structure of the company
(v) Liabilities of the members and share holders
(vi) Regarding subscription amount and related partners
(vii) General constitutional provisions and framework etc.

2. Articles of Association

Articles of association of a company as originally framed or as altered from time to time in pursuance of any law or act related to it. This document is a bye-laws or rules or regulation that governs the operation and management of its internal affairs and the conduct of its business.

Contents

Articles usually contains and provisions related particularly to internal matters of business and operational aspects for conducting the company management. They provide different informations and develop a platform of communication in company organization. They are given here as:

(i) Calls on shares
(ii) Share capital structure
(iii) Transmission of shares
(iv) Transfer of shares
(v) Alteration of capital
(vi) Conversion of shares into stock
(vii) Accounts and audits
(viii) Provisions of meetings
(ix) Right and liabilities of members
(x) Dividends and reserves
(xi) Winding up etc.

3. Prospectus

Any document described or issued as prospectus and includes any notice, circular, advertisement or other document inviting deposit from the public for the subscription or purchase of any share or debentures of a body corporate.

Contents

(i) General and introductory information of the company
(ii) Particulars and provisions of the issues of shares
(iii) Capital structure of the company
(iv) Name, address and consent of the directors
(v) Statutory informations
(vi) Management and organizational set up
(vii) Project of the company
(viii) Public issue of shares etc.
(ix) Assets and liabilities of the company.

4. Annual Accounts and Audit

Every company requires to maintain its books of accounts with respect to its business and commercial transactions. Generally, the accounts are related to trading transactions, purchase, operating expenditures, sales, group profit, net profit, capital structure, assets and liabilities etc. The audit report is also an inevitable part of company's documents. These documents are also a part of communication in company organization.

5. Register and Returns

Within different and respective provisions of the act, the company has to manage and maintain different registers, books and returns as given here:

(i) Register and index of members;
(ii) Registers of fixed deposits;
(iii) Registers of issuing shares and share holders;
(iv) Registers and index of debenture holders;
(v) Register of directors, managers and secretary;
(vi) Register of assets and liabilities;
(vii) Books of accounts;
(viii) Register of share application, allotment list, share transfer, share warrants etc.;
(ix) Register of stocks and inventories;
(x) Register of workers and employees.

6. Notice of Meeting

The notice of meetings are sent to the members, shareholders, directors and other persons who are being involved in the operation of company. It is an invitation or call letter for intimation about the meeting programes. It must always includes the following points:

(i) Name of the body/group which has to meet;

(ii) Day, date and time of the meeting;

(iii) Place and address of the area;

(iv) Agenda of the meetings;

(v) Other relevant informations.

FORMAT OF NOTICE AND AGENDA OF MEETING

TATA ENGINEERING AND LOCOMOTIVE CO. LTD.

Bombay House, 24, Homi Modi Street, Churchgate,
Mumbai-400 023

Ref. No. ________ 15th March, 2012

Mr. Mahipal Jain,
A-3/15, Mahesh Nagar
S.V. Road,
Goregaon (W)
Mumbai-400 062

Mr. Jain,

A meeting of the Board of Directors will be held on 10th April, 2012, at the registered office of the company at 2 P.M. THE AGENDA for the meeting is enclosed. Please be present at the meeting.

Yours Sincerely,

P.A. Thakore
(Secretary)

Encl. : Agenda

Items No.	Particular
1.	To confirm the minutes of the last meeting.
2.	To grant leave of absence of Mr. Rajive Mehta and Mr. Satish Verma.
3.	To produce list of accounts for payment and sign the cheques for payment.
4.	To approve transfer and transmission of shares.
5.	To put the proposal to appoint Messrs. Surdiwala and Sons as agent in Mumbai.
6.	To fix the date of the next meeting.

R.R. Mehta
Chairman

The notice of the meeting must be sent well in advance as per the requirements and well established customer. The public company and other voluntary organizations use a legal form of notice for general body meetings. The notice is accompanied by the agenda for the proposed meeting and the minutes of the previous meetings.

7. Agenda

Agenda is a list of items to be discussed at the meeting. It is usually sent with the notice of the meeting. The subject matter of it, may depend upon the types of business, working situation, proposed tasks and programmes, future related policies etc.

The agenda begins with the consequent approval of minutes, because the minutes of the previous meeting must be approved and signed by the present members. The items may be written in the agenda or in greater detail as approval of minutes of previous meeting.

Different organizations use different styles of writing the items in the agenda. They may use an informal style and describe the items in short, while some use a very formal and describe in details.

8. Minutes

The different aspects and items taken as decision at a formal meeting is known as minutes. Minutes are the official record of work done and decisions taken at the meeting of members. All the organization and committees have to maintain a record of meeting. According to the Act, every company must cause minutes of all proceedings of every meeting of its members. The details given below are an essential part of minutes and must always be included.

Contents of the minutes

(i) Name of the organization;

(ii) Nature and objectives of the meeting;

(iii) Day, date, time and place of the meeting;

(iv) Name of the chairman of the meeting;

(v) Name of members present; (List attached)

(vi) Name of persons who were invited;

(vii) Coverage of the topics on which discussions were held;

(viii) Decisions taken if any;

(ix) Leave of absence to those who are not present.

9. Workers Register

It is also an important register concerning the workers as employed in company. The contents of it are given here:

(i) Workers name and address;

(ii) Name of the section/department;

(iii) Nature of job/work
(iv) Date of appointment
(v) Status of wages and allowances
(vi) Provision of different facilities

Table 7: Statement of Supporting Documents in Company Management and their Role for Communicative Means, Style and Behaviour

There are several documents as listing here that are more or less useful to provide different facts & informations toward company management. They are so called as communicative means & methods to contribute in a wide range of communication. These are as given here:

Supporting Documents	Communicative Means, Styles and Behaviour (Provide informations)
1. Memorandum of Association	- Constitutional expression - Identification for existence
2. Articles of Association	- Internal facts and norms for working - Internal counselling
3. Prospectus	- Offer - Publicity - Advertisement
4. Annual Accounts and Audits	- Factual status - Material facts
5. Registers and Returns	- Legal evidence - Facts
Supporting Documents	**Communicative Means, Styles and Behaviour**
6. Notice of Meetings	- Information - Group message
7. Agenda	- Proposals - Intentions
8. Minutes	- Approvals - Future actions
9. Workers' Register	- Informative records - Internal records
10. Register and Record of Functional Departments	- Informative records - Material facts - Internal records
11. Resolutions	- Decisions - Future plan - Explanatory media

10. Register and Records of Functional Departments

In company organization there are several working functional departments. So there consolidated record may also be maintained at the office or central place of the company. The departments are production, inventories, maintenance, finance, purchase, accounts, sales, personnel and marketing etc.

11. Resolutions

The resolutions are also an essential part of integrated information process in a company organization. The motion or the intentions may be developed in the form of resolution. It denotes some approval to be communicated to different members of the company. Briefly, the example are given here as:

(i) It was resolved that Mr. Ram Sahai be and is hereby appointed as director.

(ii) It was resolved that secretary be and is hereby authorized to declare a share profit of 40% to shareholders.

(iii) The progress report for Jan., 2012 was presented.

(iv) The next meeting was fixed for Jan., 2013.

As such, all these documents as laid down in company management, are providing direct or indirect some way or means of communication among different partners and segments of company organization. The document itself a source or media of information which communicate the goal-oriented things to the others.

Questions

(a) Short Questions

(i) Give four names of documents in Company Management.

(ii) Define Memorandum of Association.

(iii) How does the 'Agenda' might be helpful in communication?

(iv) Give four names of registers and returns which are essential to make information process.

(v) Define Prospectus.

(b) Descriptive Questions

(i) Describe in brief the documents of Company Management and also state their supporting role for communication.

(ii) Define the prospectus and describe its role for making a better communication.

●●●

10 Chapter

Employment Communication

In the field of employment as well as job market, there are several interactions found among the employers, business classes, trading organizations and employees as well as various job seekers. The means and methods of communication are followed in employment scenario which provide some worthwhile informations and facts to the parties concern. These bias of communication develop the attention, interest, desires and actions among those persons who are involved in employment scenario.

OBJECTIVES OF EMPLOYMENT COMMUNICATION

- To make job phenomenon in employment scenario;
- To show and analyze the need and requirement of employees and workers;
- To determine the considerable factors duly effects the job and its performance;
- To display the expected skills and qualification to be needful for a job;
- To show the qualifications, achievements, hobbies and other contributions;
- To prepare the solicited and unsolicited applications for jobs;
- To create and develop the job market in multidimensional form and structure.

METHODS AND MEANS OF COMMUNICATION IN EMPLOYMENT SCENARIO

In order to develop the employment scenario, there are several methods and means of communication to incurred in it. Some of the important means are as under:

I. Job Advertisement

Advertisement is a non personal presentation and promotion of ideas by an identified sponsor. When a concern communicate the society or a specified group of persons for select or recruit some persons, that is called vacancy for a particular or some general posts. The job advertising is non-personal, which develop and introduce employment environment, originate new job markets and to enhance new working and occupational scenarios within a wide range of job market.

Main aspects of job advertising

1. It creates attention and develops the values towards the needs and requirements of employees or workers for certain jobs;
2. It creates conviction values to make trust and devotion for job performance;
3. It shows the learning values by which the methods, systems and norms are designated and shows the working process in brief to the job seekers.

The advertisement can be given by the concern or employers in written form through different methods of communication.

II. Writing Resume

It is an important part in employment communication. It shows and analyze what the application have to offer *i.e.* characteristics, skill, capabilities for performing a particular job value and interest. It also emphasise the working independability and nature as to be needful for applicants. It shows the nature and requirement of an organization as per the needs or expectations of employees on the employers' view points, the aims of the resume to find out the interest of employees and try to get an interview table.

Table 8 : Showing the Different Contents as Applicable in the Format of Resume

Those persons who required some job or want to enter in employment market can write down the resume through major contents as given here:

Major Contents of Resume	Description
1. Job	1. Here we can mention the name of the job. 2. Sub part of the job, if any.
2. Name and Addresses	1. Write down your name with surname. 2. Give local and postal address.
3. Career Objectives	1. Your career objectives should indicate in context of the job. 2. Your personal objectives should indicate for better performance in the job.
4. Summary of Qualifications	1. Generally the qualification is long and varied. So we must summarize them, in tabulation form. 2. To highlight the useful and strong points. 3. It must be brief and in short form.

Contd...

Major Contents of Resume	Description
5. Education	1. For education status, it is needful to display them particularly at the initial stage. 2. All the stages and levels of education should be included in it.
6. Co-curricular Activities	1. All the other activities should be shown as participated by the candidate. 2. It shows the participation in Games, Sports, NCC, NSS, Rovers and other voluntary services.
7. Work Experience	1. Work experience as hold by the candidate with some details as name of the job, concern, nature of work, how long worked there with duties and responsibilities. 2. Any achievement honours and contributions as signified by candidate.
8. Other Qualities	1. Team spirit. 2. Leadership. 3. Specking, writing and tutoring etc. 4. Creative projects. 5. Motivational qualities.
9. Personal Data	1. Candidates' interest and hobbies. 2. Language known. 3. Physical and Health status. 4. Body language.
10. References	1. Generally there is a need to show three or five references for personal identification. 2. The designation, telephone numbers and e-mail etc. should be provided.

Contd...

Major Contents of Resume	Description
11. Supporting Documents	1. List should be prepared for supporting documents with the resume. 2. Mention to offer to present these documents on request.

KINDS OF ATTENTION IN RESUME

I. *The chronological attention*

It shows the work performance historically in date and time wise order.

II. *The functional attention*

It focuses on the area of strong performance or most competencies.

III. *The targeted attention*

It shows the qualification and capabilities for a specific job or work or a specified area.

III. Application Letters

The application letters are written by candidates when they want a job. This letter as well as along with it, the resume must show and emphasize to the employers in such a way that they can understand how the candidate it beneficial to the organization. It should be more like a persuasive letter. It basically aims to get the interview letter from the employer. It must reflect the personal style, skills, capabilities, confidence and also it conveys the desire to join the prospective organization.

TYPES OF APPLICATION FOR JOB

There are two types of application letters as given here:

1. *Solicited Letters*

   This type of application is based on the response to an advertisement for job.

2. *Unsolicited Letters*

   This type of application is based on the own initiative by job seekers or writers. Here, there is no any responses arising from employers' side.

Format for Application Letter
The contents of application letter are as given here–
(Solicited form)

The Reliance Communications,
Deep Plaza,
Mahal Road, Agra

Reference - As per your advt. dt. ....

Subject - For the post of supervisor

Sir,

With reference and subject as mentioned above, I would like to offer my services for the post of supervisor at your centre. My enclosed details will reveal that I have some of needful qualities and interest that will greatly help the credentials of organization. I enclose herewith my resume for your consideration.

I will be grateful for an opportunity to serve under your kind perusal.

Thanking you Sir.

Yours faithfully

ABC

Encl. Personal Bio Data (Resume)

IV. References

Different people who wants to get needful jobs, they apply for it. Some of the persons who provide different jobs to a mass number of people are required to get the social status, behaviour, working performance and creditable position for those people who apply or required to get some jobs. In general, where the prospective employer has no clue about the candidate, it is necessary to obtain, that is called 'References' or a 'Testimonials'. It denotes about the candidate's integrity, ability and character etc. In these documents, the candidate shows the name and address of some reliable persons who has long and standing relations with the prospective candidate. The employer or the company has to verify about the status and reliability of candidate from the reliable persons.

V. Testimonials

It is an open document and without having any address to anyone, that shows the skills and abilities of candidate for a particular job. It is more or less the nature of a certificate that verified the character, behaviour and qualifications of the candidate in whose favour it is prepared. It can be taken from an ex-employer in which some satisfactory and pleasant remarks are given about the work performance. It is like a certificate, and so, should not be written in the letter format. These are also important part for the interaction of communication in employment scenario.

VI. Interview Letters

At the employer side, after getting different applications from job seekers, there is an important step to call them for face to face interaction from any organization. The applicants invited to attend a common meeting in that the queries are solved and they arrived at the conclusion *i.e.* called interview. From the employer side, the members who taking the interview may ask some common questions like the job oriented targets, knowledge about job performance, efficiency, skills for jobs, past experience, working norms and other terms etc. The interview atmosphere should be in congenial and harmonious way and they ultimately support and motivate the candidate.

VII. Appointment Letters

Desh Pandey & Power Stream Ltd.
Badar Pur, Lucknow

Dear Mr. Anand,

This is with reference to your application dated 2nd July, 2010 and the subsequent interview on 20th July, 2010.

I am pleased to inform you that you have been selected for the post of sales manager in our organization. You are required to contact Mr. Ajay Dev, Personnel Manager on or before 30th July, 2010. He will guide you about the nature of your duties.

The terms and conditions of your appointment are as follows:

(i) The post is a permanent one with a probation period of 6 months. Your performance will be reviewed by us and on proving satisfactory, your service will be confirmed.

(ii) Your salary has been fixed at Rs. 25,000/- p.m. and the increment on it will be Rs. 500/- p.a.

(iii) You are entitled to get all other benefits as per our norms.

(iv) A notice period of 1 months is required from either side in case of termination of services or resignation.

We wish you all the success in your future venture.

Yours faithfully

ABC

An employer writes an appointment letter to the job seekers or those candidates who have been selected for a particular job.

On behalf of the employer, the head of the personal department or any responsible person sends it in duplicate form. The selected candidates should sign one copy to show their acceptance. They can retain the other copy for their records. Some of the points to be considered while writing an appointment letter as the letter should be refered to the interview, the terms and conditions should be mentioned properly, it should express the employers' pleasures as well as with good luck wishes to the candidate for the new job.

Table 9: Showing the Contents of Appointment Letters

The contents or some of the details are mentioned in appointment letter are given here:

1. Name of the post	6. The benefit
2. The date of joining	7. The probation period
3. The working timings/schedule	8. The leave rules and process
4. The consolidate salary	9. The period of notice from either side for termination
5. The nature of work/duty	10. The designation

SALARY AND WAGES STRUCTURE

The salary and wages structure and the pay off of the employees development programme are very much near to the performance and job merits of employees. On the basis of the job evaluation and merit rating system, the components and the structure of salary and wages are being determined. It should be communicated to employees in a proper way. The components of this structure are given here:

FORMAT OF A WAGE AND SALARY STRUCTURE

The format of this structure is as under:

(i) Basic Pay and Wages
(ii) Dearness Allowance
(iii) House Rent Allowance
(iv) Other Allowances

Deductions

(i) Provident Fund
(ii) Employees Insurance
(iii) Welfare Fund
(iv) Any Other Deductions

VIII. Induction

After getting the appointment letters from employers, the appointed candidates can get the detail information about their jobs. This induction methods to develop the interaction with candidates may provide the nature of job, methods to perform job, job specifications and required aspects of job for better performance.

Questions

(a) Short Questions

(i) What are the objectives of Employment Communications?

(ii) What are the main aspects of job advertising?

(iii) What is meant by references?

(iv) Define the salary and Wages structure.

(v) Briefly state some of the important points to be considered in Appointment letter.

(vi) Why do we need to write a Resume?

(vii) What points must be kept in mind while writing an Application Letter?

(viii) What is the solicited and unsolicited letters?

(ix) What is Induction?

(b) Descriptive Questions

(i) Define appointment letter. Draft a letter intimating the appointment to a person who has been appointed for the post of an accountant in an office.

(ii) Draft a resume, keeping in mind all the needful contents that have to be included.

(iii) Draft an application to Mafat Lal & Group Ltd., Surat for the post of a lady receptionist-cum-typist-cum-telephone operator, specially emphasizing your good command over English, your knowledge of the job of handling PABX/Telex and your dignified personality.

●●●

Part - IV

Management and Communications

11 Chapter

Management and Communication

CONCEPT OF MANAGEMENT

'Management is the art of getting things done through and with people in formally organized groups. It is the art of creating the environment in which people can perform as individuals and yet cooperate towards attainment of group goals.' Managerial activities involved variety fragmentation, brevity and a large volume of work to be performed quickly. In global business environment, the communication has become the key role for doing managerial task and performance & it becomes a largest and dynamic transforming bases for management excellences.

KEY MANAGERIAL ROLES

In any organization, the managerial roles have been an important and decisional part. The key role must have to identify for getting some better and productive result, specifically in the field of communication.

Henry Mintzberg has identified different role common to the work of all managers. They are summarized into three groups as given here:

1. Role of Interpersonal
2. Role of Informational
3. Role of Decisional

1. Role of Interpersonal

Managers deal with the subordinates to get things done with their help. For this, in any organization they have to interact and maintain good relations with them. They provide their roles such as:

(i) Figurehead
(ii) Leader
(iii) Liaison

2. Role of Informational

It is very important for managers to communicate effectively in order to get things done. Receiving continuously information from various sources and transit only the desired information. They provide their informative role in any organization as:

(i) Monitor
(ii) Disseminator
(iii) Spokesperson

3. **Role of Decisional**

Decision making is inherent to the job of manager. The managers have to take a large number and wide range of decisions daily to run the organization. They provide their decisional role in any organization as:

(i) Entrepreneur
(ii) Disturbance handler
(iii) Resources allocator
(iv) Negotiator

The above key managerial roles are being beneficial to develop an effective process and environment for communication.

MANAGERIAL FUNCTIONS AND COMMUNICATION

It is an utmost need to determine the managerial functions specifically to implement the objectives and programmes of the organization. Here, a brief note is involved to describe the functions and the assisting role of communication for implementing them are also given here:

1. **Planning**

According to **G.R. Terry** – "Planning is a method or technique of looking ahead a constructive reviewing of future needs so that present action can be adjusted in view of the established goals." It is an objective based process and it has a wide scope which is basically based on decision making process. The different means and medias of communication might be beneficial to assist the informative aspects for properly implementing the different techniques of planning like objectives, policies, procedures, rules, methods, programmes, schedules and strategies etc.

2. **Decision Making**

According to **R.S. Davar** – "Decision making can be defined as the selection based on some criteria of one behaviour alternatives from two or more possible alternatives." It includes to analyze the problem to know the environmental factors, to find out best alternatives solution, to determine the accountabilities, to evaluate the alternative and find out selection of the best solutions. The methods of decision making are intuition, opinion viewpoints, experience, practical viewpoints, model building, standards, operational research and linear programming etc. which may be implemented through proper communication system.

3. **Organizing**

According to **Theo Haimann** – "Organizing is defining and grouping of activities and establishing the authority relationship among them. It is a group of persons, a functional process, a means for coordinating the rights and duties among people. The means of communication are being able to encourage different motivational principles of organization like principles of unity of direction, scalar chain, team spirit, continuity, balancing, stability, morale, human relations and sound communication.

4. **Direction**

According to **Theo Haimann** – Directing consists of the process and techniques use in issuing instruction and making certain operations that are carried on as originally planned, it is a pervasive function, it has many activities and process, it provide working parameter, it is related with human elements and motivation, it helps in leadership, it has some useful components or techniques like orders and instruction, supervision, decision making, effective communication and controls etc. All these aspects depend upon effective communication.

5. **Coordination**

According to **Henry Fayol** – "To coordinate is to harmonize all the activities of a concern in order to facilitate working and its order to facilitate working and its success." It has due importance towards making mutual cooperation, overall accomplishment to reduce difference, to raise moral, to arranged sequence and develop a wide range of mutual combinations. Coordination is based on some fundamental principles like reciprocal relationships, direct contact, continues process, team spirit, time suited and dynamism etc.

6. **Leadership**

According to **Robert Albansese** – "Managerial leadership is that behaviour that elicits voluntary follows behaviour beyond that associated with required performance on a job." Effective leadership is an important function of management, which is based on an appropriate communication systems. It aims to develop common efforts, high morale, managerial excellences, to develop better organizational behaviour, to create confidence and enthusiasm etc.

7. **Motivation**

According to **W.G. Scott** – "Motivation means a process of stimulating people to action to accomplish desired goals." It aims to motivate people for maximizing work performance, to improve the efficiency of workers, to provide work recognition, devotion builds morale and more belongingness among workers. It is based on the principles of team spirit, human relations, participation, objectivity, proper right and duties, feeling of security, personality development and achieving opportunities.

8. **Communication**

According to **Keith Davis** – "Communication is the process of passing informations from one person to another and understanding. More or less communication is a part of entire management and the role of it can provide some proper and concurrent benefits in management process. The important role of communication can be stated in different areas like planning, organization, decision making, coordination, motivation and control etc.

9. Control

According to **Philip Kotler** – "Control is the process of taking steps to bring actual results and desired closer together. Within the process of control, the managerial roles are very important particularly at the implementation of planning, valuation of work performance, proper coordination and making some corrective actions.

SIGNIFYING ROLE OF COMMUNICATION FOR MANAGEMENT

Communication is the foremost and needful aspect for managerial and organizing the enterprise. The means and methods of communication have some signifying role for managers at every sphere of their task. The dynamic and signifying role of communication in the field of management are as given here:

1. For Effective Planning

The role of communication is needful to provide different information, facts and data for the preparation of plan network in any concern. The communication is needful at every stage for implementation of planning.

2. For Forecasting

The role of forecasting is needful to develop future oriented task and as such the role of communication is very important to make the process of forecasting. Informative network is going on with the new technology of MIS towards performing the research for future oriented task.

3. To Motivate Employees

In order to motivate the employees, there is a need to aquaint them with motives, desires, expectations which depends upon the informations and reports arising out from the means of communication. It is also needful to implement the methods of motivation for the interest of employees.

4. For Sound Decision

For making effective and rational process of decision making, the methods of communication has provided various facts and information which are needful for sound decision. In fact the decision making process totally depends upon the methods and means of communication.

5. For Effective Leadership

With the qualitative effective and availability of needful information, the efficient leadership can be developed. The means of communication can be able to develop the sense of discipline, high morale, team spirit, effective direction and work accomplishment etc.

6. For Effective Organizational Structure

For efficient management system, there is a need to determine and establish optimum organizational structure within the work assignment, mutual relations among persons, determine the rights and duties & all depend upon effective communication.

7. **For Establishment Effective Coordination**

   On the basis of facts, informations and other messages, the coordination may be established in the concern. Communication may develop the integrated and interrelationship patterns in management.

8. **For Implementing the Principles of Management**

   All the different principles which gives best suited directions to the concern, can be determined and implemented through the means of communication.

9. **To Build Morale**

   With the help of different means of communication, manager might be able to get some useful views, ideas and sentiments so that on these bases they can create some motivational aspects. It will be helpful to build morale among employees.

10. **Establishing the Democratic Management**

    The management can get all the values and other concepts for making a democratic system in the concern, through some suitable sources of communication. As such, the democratically pattern may be developed through effective communication.

11. **Establishing Mutual Cooperation**

    In any concern, communication is an important and decisional part by which a lot of cooperation can be established among different people. Different informations would be able to create trust, confidence and mutual cooperation among the people.

12. **For Effective Control System**

    There is a need of proper communication for making an effective control system. On the basis of the information available the evaluation of work done as per the norms or standards can be possible.

13. **For Redressal of Complaints and Grievances**

    In any concern the complaints and grievances in any organization can be solved through proper media and techniques of communication.

14. **For Builds Human Relations**

    With the help of communication, a manager can be able to get different factors to affect the human side of the employees. With some suitable means of communication, there is a great possibility to establish good human relations with employees.

15. **Establishing Relations with External Partners**

    The means of communication can provide the plans, objectives and other needful aspects of the concern with the externals partners. By it the relations can be developed with them properly.

16. Helpful in Change Management

The management can get proper informations about the present and potential changes of business, so communication is helpful to manage the avenues of changes and its consequent effect.

17. Operating the Functional Management

The means of communication can provide different informations and try to implement proper different functional areas of management.

Table 10: Showing the Managerial Functions with their Basic Aspects and Role of Means/Media of Communication Towards Assisting Them

While studying the role of communication towards different functional areas of management. Here some of the basic and foremost means or media are being evolved stating to provide basic assistance to different managerial function. The means or media most suitable as provide some needful assistance towards executing the basic aspects of managerial functions are given here:

Functions of Management	Basic Aspects	Means/Media Communication
1. Planning	(i) Management by objectives (ii) Policies, programmes, Rules and Procedure (iii) Strategies	- Downward communication - Oral and written communication - Internal and external communication
2. Decision making	(i) Goal orientation (ii) Best alternatives (iii) Commitments (iv) Analysis and evaluating resources	- Oral and written communication - Formal & internal communication
3. Organization	(i) Rights and responsibilities (ii) Organization behaviour (iii) Human approaches	- Downward communication - Horizontal communication - Group level interaction

Contd...

Functions of Management	Basic Aspects	Means/Media Communication
4. Direction	(i) Effective leadership (ii) Uniformity of objectives (iii) Proper integration (iv) Effective communication	- Downward communication - Written communication - Informal communication
5. Coordination	(i) Mutual cooperation (ii) Integrated relations	- Informal communication - Horizontal communication
6. Leadership	(i) Direction abilities (ii) Group efforts and team spirit (iii) Behaviour approaches (iv) Confidence, decision making abilities and loyalty	- Oral communication - Informative communication
7. Motivation	(i) Team spirit (ii) Loyalty and belongingness	- Informative communication - Informal communication
8. Communication	(i) Effective transmission (i) Individual & Group Interaction	- All the effective means and methods which provide managerial excellences.
9. Control	(i) Role of norms and standards (ii) Evaluation of work performance (iii) Assistance in work and not interference	- Upward & Downward communication - Information communication

As such, in order to make some excellences and making innovative viewpoints, the role and means of communication is necessary. The different signifying role of communication can provide a better platform for management and its allied activities.

CHALLENGING PART OF COMMUNICATION

Here, some of the problems or challenges are arising out of the communication process within the management scenario. These are as given here:

1. Undesirable, unsound, doubtful objectives and goals can create the problem.
2. Some of the listening obstacles like language problem, speedy sound and other physical barriers etc.
3. The individual and group difference due to different demographical factors.
4. Negligent behaviour of the top level management.
5. Narrow and self centered ideas, viewpoints and attitudes of persons.
6. Complicated, undesirable and wide organizational structure.
7. Lack of confidence, trust and belongingness and
8. Ignorance about modern technique of communication

PERSPECTIVES

In order to properly execute the basic aspects, necessary functions and processes of management in any organization, there is a need to develop some essential work environment by means of communication or some basis of interaction. The perspective means are given here:

(i) Informal Organization

The managers should develop the informal relations with employees with the help of informal communication.

(ii) Individual and Group Behaviour

There is a need to make some fruitful interaction between individual and group behaviour. The process and means of communication will develop a right platform for it.

(iii) Develop the Motivational Aspects

The managers can develop some sort of motivational aspects for entire employees with the help of perspective communication.

(iv) Develop Managerial Skills

The managers can develop their knowledge and skills to adopt the new and innovative techniques of mass communication.

(v) Effective Coordination

The managers should develop the coordination among the task and employees of organization. The coordinated efforts by means of communication is essential for not only managerial task but to perform the communication process properly.

(vi) Better Conduct and Behaviour

The managers should develop better conduct and behaviour with the entire part of organization. It is possible by means of communication and different sort of interactions.

Questions

(a) Short Questions

(i) Define the Informational role of Management.

(ii) Define any two functions of Management.

(iii) Define the Motivation.

(iv) Give any two signifying role of Communication for Management.

(v) Give any four problems or limitations of Communication for Management.

(vi) Give the names of the means/media of communication for Planning and Control.

(b) Descriptive Questions

(i) Define Management. What are the functions of Management?

(ii) Analysis the signifying role of Communication for performing the managerial functions.

(iii) Describe the means/media for assisting role towards executing the functions of Management.

(iv) Describe the perspectives for developing managerial role through the means of Communication.

●●●

12 Chapter

Functional Area of Business/Management and Communication System

The study of managerial communication system of different specialized as well as functional area of business is an important part. Within the modern business there is emerged a new trends of specialization, value creation, data based decision process, skilled business ventures, coordination and professionalization and as such, it is needful to frame out a network of functional communication system in an organization.

According to **Joseph J. Massie** – "Functional Management is a specialized branch of general management."

According to **Stoner and Freeman** – "The functional manager is responsible for only one organizational activity such as production, finance, marketing or sales."

The functional area of business have the different functional parts in that the study of communication is needful.

CHARACTERISTICS OF FUNCTIONAL MANAGEMENT

The main characteristics of functional management are given here:

(i) The concept and tasks of functional management is based on the principle of specialization.

(ii) The different work are divided into various small part or segments which have some special features.

(iii) It denotes the managerial and operational tasks to perform specialized area or a part of a segment.

(iv) The structural division of organization is based on specialized work or a specific task etc.

(v) The functional management have a wide scope or working area due to involvement of different specialized sector in it.

(vi) The different specialized area or respective departments are performed their task under the leadership of functional manager.

(vii) There is a mutual coordination between the general manager and different respective functional managers.

(viii) All the functional departments are inter-dependents and have some integrated relations with each other.

(ix) There are also different managerial levels in the functional department.

(x) The functional managers have the double role as firstly they have the leading capacity at their department and secondly they provide needful suggestions or specialized services on behalf of their department to the top management.

(xi) The functional departments have the specialized technical knowledge and skills.

(xii) They follow all the processes, methods and principles same as followed by the general management.

OBJECTIVES OF COMMUNICATION SYSTEM IN FUNCTIONAL MANAGEMENT

The communication system has the foremost part and provide different informative services to various functional management. Its objectives are briefly stating here:

(i) It assists the functional management to manage the different managerial functions.

(ii) To provide needful informations for performing the specialized work at their level.

(iii) To provide different methods and techniques to different functional management for their work performance.

(iv) To make mutual cooperation and coordination between general management and different functional management.

(v) To provide needful assistance for taking speedy and in proper timely decisions.

(vi) To provide new avenues of research and development in the concern.

(vii) To provide new and innovative systems and process for informational structure in the functional management:

DIFFERENT FUNCTIONAL AREAS OF MANAGEMENT AND INFORMATION SYSTEM

It is needful to study the creative role of communication systems and their applicability into the different functional areas of management. The applicability of the means and systems of communication with some perspective results in the functional areas of management are given here:-

I. Production Management and Communication System

Production management is an important and specific part of the entire management. It perform all the managerial functions like planning, decision making, organizing, coordination, direction and control for the production and manufacturing process in any concern. It aims to determine and prepare product planning, play layout, select the production systems, the requirement of raw material, equipments, machineries and different infrastructural facilities.

INTEGRATED COMMUNICATION SYSTEM

Within the production planning and there are some internal and external aspects which provide technological and decisional role. The communication system as an integral part, also provide some needful contribution to these aspects and as such the composition of them are known as integrated system. The main aspects in this system as assisting by communications are given here:

(i) Research and Hypothesis

There is a foremost and basic task of production management in conducting research and investigation about product, machineries, employees, market and technical aspects. The means and media of communication provide various informations and helps in these research and hypothesis process. On this basis the quality, design, features, size and quantity etc. can get a proper position in this area.

(ii) Standards and Norms

The communication system has the obligatory role to collect the informations about expectations, buying motives, demand forecasting, consumers' behaviour. On this basis the standard, goals and norms can be determined.

(iii) Stock Information System

The communication system has the stock information system in that the facts and informations related to raw materials are included. Here, the informations about the sources of raw material, requirement of raw material, order processing time, safety stock, maintenance cost and other technical aspects are included in it.

(iv) Product Planning

On the basis of different informations carried out by communication system are product, installed capacity, production processes and perspective way to get better technological level. The determining the planning and implementation of the components of planning are also an important part in communication system.

(v) Manufacturing Process and Work Performance

On the basis of the informations as carried out by communication process, the manufacturing process can be done properly. This performance part is also an inevitable part of communication and thus the implementation of production control can be possible easily.

Model-2

SHOWING THE INTEGRATED COMMUNICATION SYSTEM IN PRODUCTION MANAGEMENT

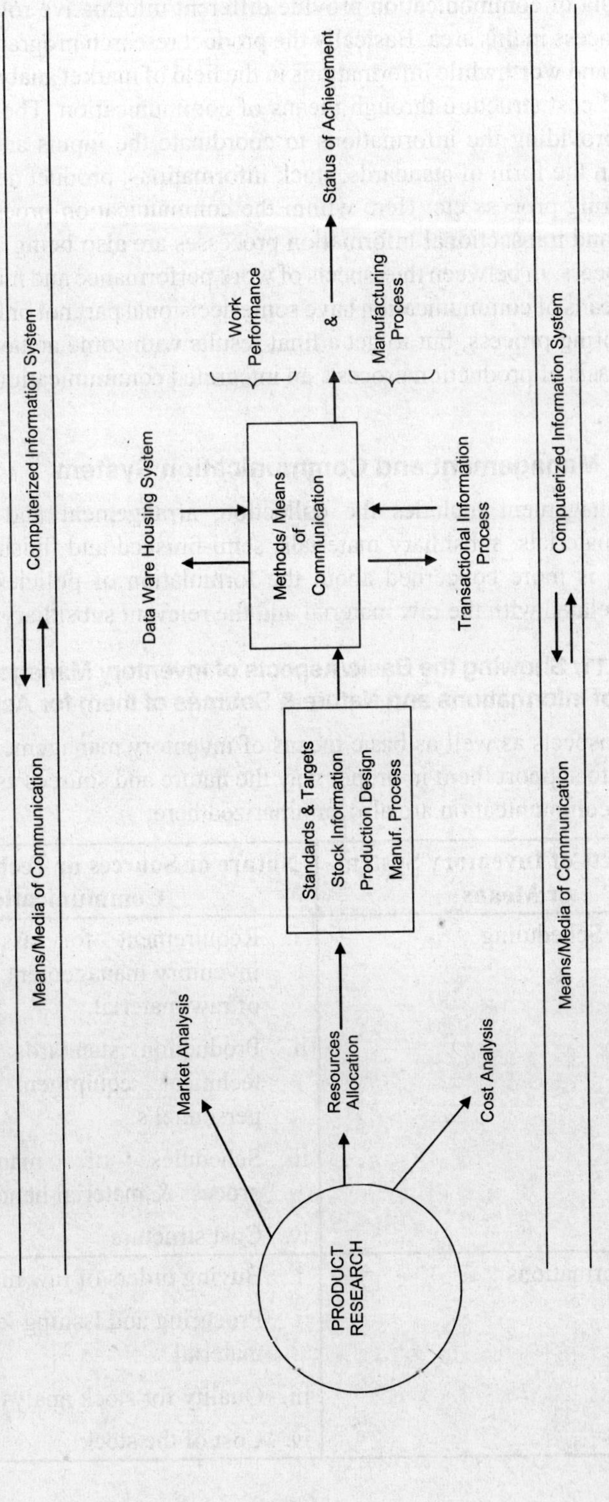

The model depicts that within the scenario of production management the means or media of communication provide different informative role to perform the overall process in this area. Basically the product research programme provide the analytical and worthwhile informations in the field of market analysis, resource allocation and cost structure through means of communication. The information systems are providing the informations to coordinate the inputs and outputs of product task in the form of standards, stock informations, product design as well as manufacturing process etc. Here within the communication process, the data warehousing and transactional information processes are also being an important part in this process. In between the aspects of work performance and manufacturing process the means of communication have some decisional part not only to proceed the manufacturing process, but to get a final results with some achievements. As such, on the basis of production process, an integrated communication system can be evolved.

II. Inventory Management and Communication System

Inventory management includes the collection, arrangement and managerial task for raw materials, subsidiary materials, semi-finished and finished products etc. This area is more concerned about the formulation of policies, plans and programmes related with the raw material and the relevant subsidiary materials.

Table - 11: Showing the Basic/Aspects of Inventory Management Concerning of Informations and Nature & Sources of them for Assisting in It

The different aspects as well as basic means of inventory management are given here. In order to support them in proper way the nature and sources as well as the techniques of communication are also summarized here:

Bases/Aspects of Inventory System or Means	Nature or Sources or Techniques of Communication
I. Production Scheduling	i. Requirement for assisting the inventory management and nature of raw material. ii. Production standards for time, technical equipment and for personnel's. iii. Schedules of manufacturing process & material handling iv. Cost structure
II. Stock Informations	i. Buying orders of raw material ii. Procuring and Issuing level of raw material iii. Quality for stock analysis iv. Cost of the stock

Contd...

Bases/Aspects of Inventory System or Means	Nature or Sources or Techniques of Communication
	v. Processing time vi. Role of TPS in stock management
III. Stock Accounts	i. Stock vouchers ii. Carriage receipts iii. Stock accounts & registers iv. Data warehousing
IV. Production Control	i. Data support ii. Result analysis iii. Findings of variances iv. Stock verifications v. Corrective actions
V. Techniques of Stock Control	i. Order point techniques ii. Stock process scheduling iii. Break even analysis iv. Cost Control devices v. Inventory Control devices vi. A.B.C. analysis

The model depicts that the process of stock information system has started with the role of MIS which can get the stock information from various sources of operating management. It develop the process of data transmitting in the form of data processing and data analysis. Then different core aspects specially production schedule, stock information (updated) stock accounting and stock control can get their operating position. The identification and utilization of information is being done for better way of stock management.

III. Financial Management and Communication System

According to **Howard and Upton** – "Financial Management is the application of planning and control to the financial functions".

Financial management is indispensable organ and have a wide scope of business management. It is more analytical and less descriptive. It helps the top management in determining policies and plans as well as in decision making also. Today the business performance is measured on the basis of financial results.

FINANCIAL INFORMATION SYSTEM

Within the framework of financial management, a managerial information system has developed with the supporting aspects of data storage and data analytical

Model No. 3

Showing the Stock information system in inventory management

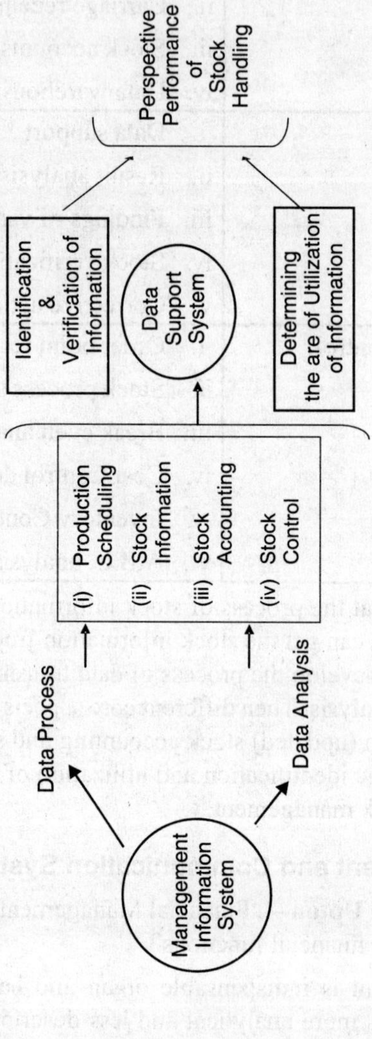

processes. In this field, a major part of information processing is based on MIS & different modules of software. This system may be helpful to provide different communication services. The services as provided by it are given here:

(i) To determine policies and plans for financial management;
(ii) To help in allocation of resources;
(iii) To help in managing cash and assets;
(iv) To help in financial control;
(v) To make coordination with other department of the concern;
(vi) To measure and control over the cost;
(vii) To analyze and evaluate the financial sources and their utilization;
(viii) To help the investors and other institutions;
(ix) To help in tax and audit management for the concern.

Model - 4
SHOWING THE INTEGRATED FINANCIAL INFORMATION SYSTEM (Components)

In order to perform the functions and responsibilities of financial management the different components can provide the data and information as per the requirement of this management. The name of the components are given here:

Information - Flow

Information Flow | Information Flow

I. *Production Planning and Development*
1. Project Performance
2. Standards
3. Cost Analysis

II. *Finance and Accounting Operations*
1. Plans and procedures
2. Cash management
3. Resources allocation

III. *Personnel Management*
1. HR Developments
2. HR Costs
3. Training and Development

IV. *Capital Management*
1. Capital Budgeting
2. Capital Structure
3. Capital gains and expenditures

V. *Marketing Management*
1. Buying and selling transactions
2. Sales analysis
3. Market segments

VI. *Investment Management*
1. Investment - analysis
2. Risk Analysis
3. Profitability Analysis

FINANCIAL PLANNING, PERFORMANCE AND CONTROL

The model depicts that integrated financial information system has the composition of the role of different functional departments. It is a procedural frame work aims to make the integrated relations with the other counterparts. The process of data collection and data interpretations are being going on through the supporting task and contribution of each functional department. All the areas are providing their data and informations specifically related to financial management and as such these informations are used by this integrated systems.

Table 12: Showing the Means/Media of Informations in the form of Documents Used in Financial Management

In financial management the means or documents for transmitting the relevant informations are listed below:

(i)	Cash receipts
(ii)	Vouchers
(iii)	Financial records
(iv)	Buying and selling vouchers
(v)	Statement of funds
(vi)	Bank voucher and statement
(vii)	Cash flow statement
(viii)	Forecasted financial statements etc.
(ix)	Working capital structure
(x)	Profit and loss statement etc.

IV. Cost Management and Information System

Cost management is concerned to collect, evaluate, analyze, account and classified the expenditures relating to the activities of the concern. It deals to manage, organize, coordinate and control of all the direct and indirect components of the cost of different tasks. It includes different aspects particularly the elements of cost, cost estimation, calculation of cost, cost structure and variation between estimated cost and actual cost etc.

The model depicts that in order to make a supporting task and to provide some assisting role to the cost management, an integrated communication system can be emerged. In this system the informations can be obtained from the internal and external sources and these can be utilized at the cost centers related to different sections or departments. With the help of some support system the analysis and evaluation of the different components can be possible. Here, an important part to analyze and evaluate the estimated and actual cost can not be denied. The cost and benefit analysis is also an important part to get some perspective result in the field of cost management. The information support system can provide a lot of assistance in it.

Model - 5

SHOWING THE INTEGRATED COMMUNICATION SYSTEM IN COST MANAGEMENT

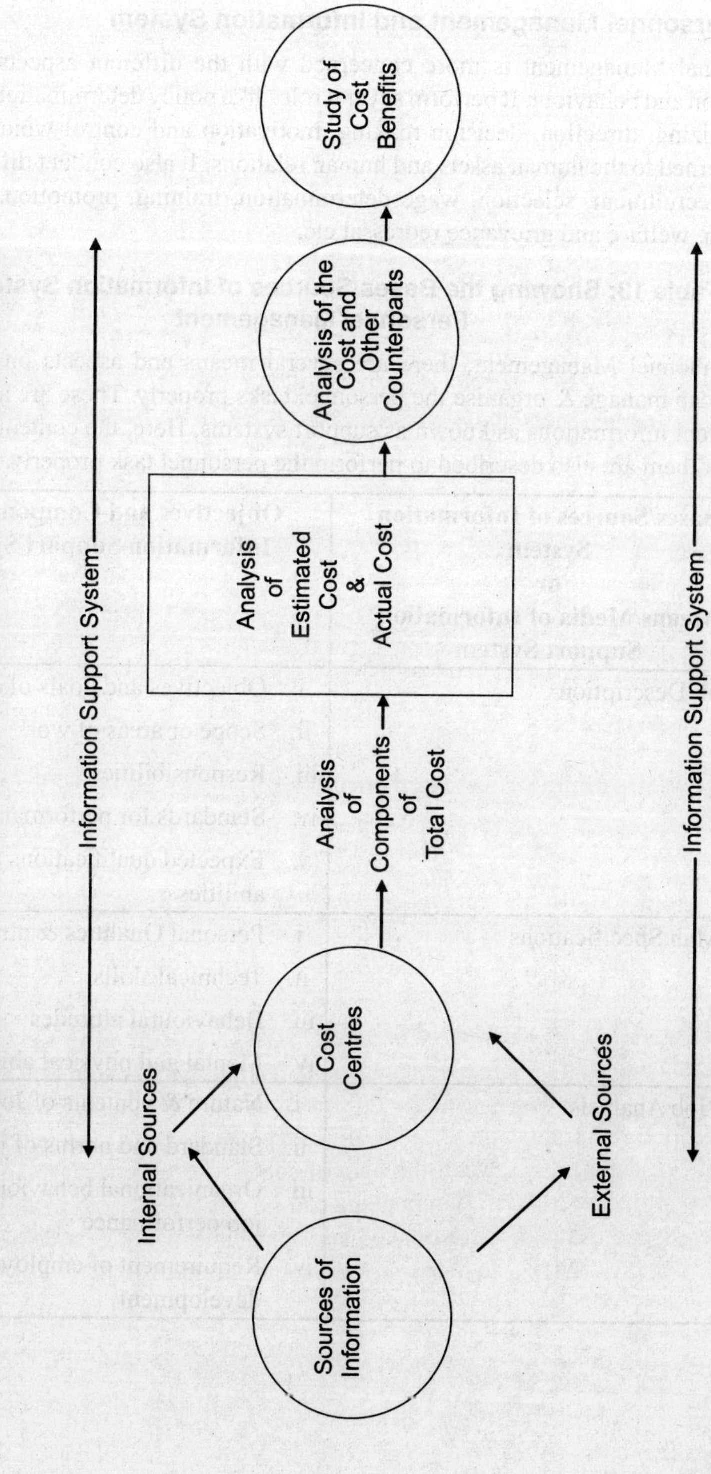

V. Personnel Management and Information System

Personal Management is more concerned with the different aspects of human relation and behaviour. It perform several roles like policy determination, planning, organizing, direction, decision making, motivation and control which are more concerned to the human assets and human relations. It also conduct different tasks like recruitment, selection, wage determination, training, promotion, demotion, health, welfare and grievance redressal etc.

Table 13: Showing the Bases/Sources of Information System for Personnel Management

In personnel Management, there are several means and aspects on which this field can manage & organise the personnel tasks properly. These are also provide different informations as known as support systems. Here, the contents as arising out of them are also described to perform the personnel task properly.

Bases/Sources of Information System or Means/Media of Information Support System	Objectives and Components of Information Support System
I. Job Description	i. Objectives and goals of a task ii. Scope or areas of work iii. Responsibilities iv. Standards for performance v. Expected qualifications and abilities
II. Man Specifications	i. Personal Qualities & attitudes ii. Technical skills iii. Behavioural attitudes iv. Mental and physical abilities
III. Job Analysis	i. Nature & contents of Job ii. Standard and norms of job iii. Organizational behaviour within job performance iv. Requirement of employees development

Bases/Sources of Information System or Means/Media of Information Support System	Objectives and Components of Information Support System
IV. Job Induction	i. Recruitment plans and programmes ii. Sources and process of selection & recruitment iii. Introduction about job & concern iv. Job performance - methods, process & supporting elements
V. Training and Development	i. Training methods & process ii. Syllabi of training iii. Organizational development
VI. Remunerative Plans	i. Wage structure ii. Fringe benefits iii. Methods of wage determination

Here, the model depicts that a communication network might be able to make a procedural way for performing the personnel functions. It may start with the personnel policies and programmes which can transmit to the Data warehousing cell *i.e.* called the human resources information mechanism. On the basis of the information as collected at this stage, several aspects of personnel management can develop and perform their roles. These aspects are also called as means or media or supporting devices to perform the personnel task or functions in proper way. According to these aspects as supported by some worthwhile informations, the procurement, organisation, utilisation & development of Human Resources can be possible properly.

VI. Office Management and Information System

Office management is a pivoted and central point of the business management. In fact, all the activities, performance, directions and policy implementation are directed and control over this focal point. It manage and maintain all the records and accounts relevant to different sections and departments of the concern.

SOURCES AND APPLICABILITY OF INFORMATIONS SYSTEM IN OFFICE MANAGEMENT

Within the information system, there are two major areas or techniques by which the information can be obtained and these sources are also the basis for the applicability of these informations in different area of office management.

Model - 6

SHOWING THE PERSONNEL/HUMAN RESOURCES INFORMATION SYSTEM

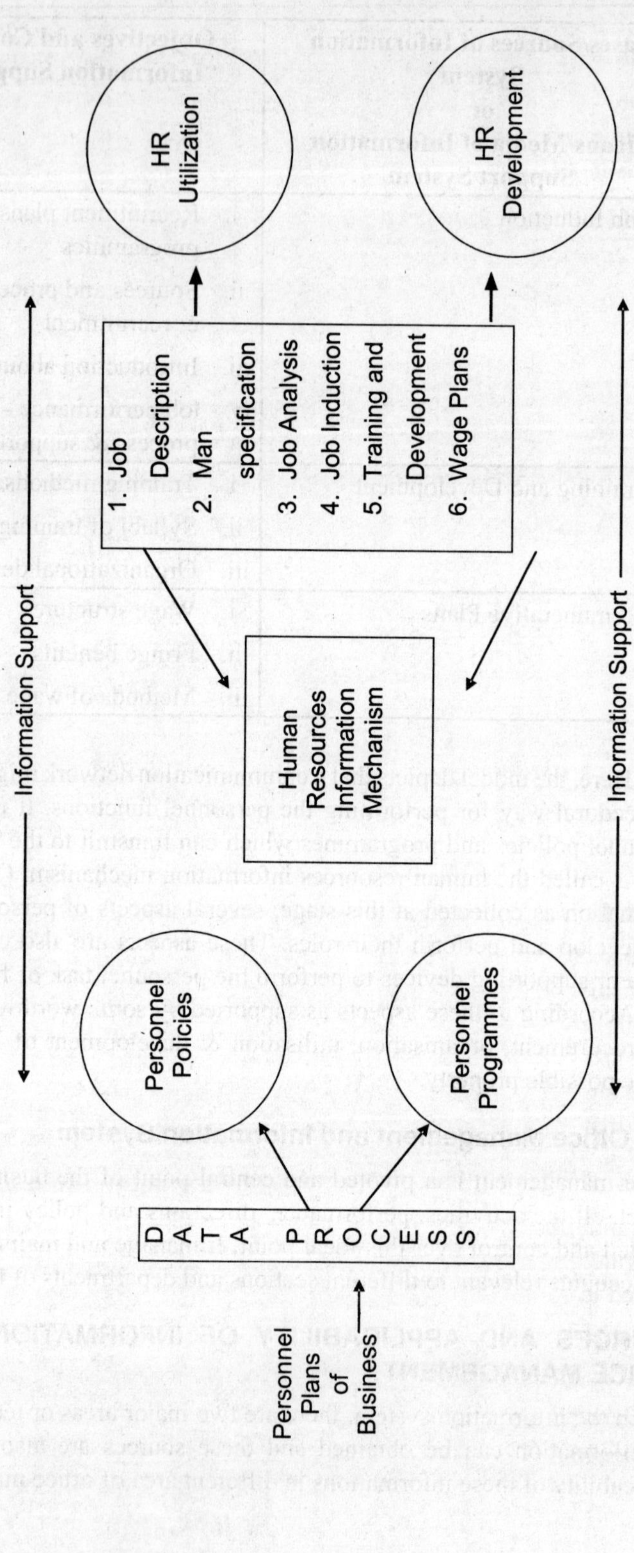

Table 14: Showing the Methods/Systems of Office Communication

There are two major methods cum sources for contribute different facts & informations to conduct & support the office management. These methods are old & new as listing here-

I. Old and Traditional Methods	II. New and Automation Systems
(i) Orders	(i) Desk Top Publishing (DTP)
(ii) Circulars	(ii) Computer Aided Design (CAD)
(iii) Office note	(iii) Electronic Bulletin Boards
(iv) Notice	(iv) Facsimile
(v) Reference letters	(v) Internet
(vi) Reports and manuals	(vi) Voice Mail
(vii) Advertisement	(vii) Electronic Mail (E-mail)
	(viii) Archival Storage
	(ix) Multimedia
	(x) Video Conferencing
	(xi) Fax
	(xii) Online Chat Tools
	(xiii) Client Server Computing

VII. Marketing Management and Communication System

Market management is a dynamic and decisional part which has an interdisciplinary approach of entire business management. It manage and conduct the planning, organizing, coordinating and control over the marketing activities. It includes the different tasks of buying and selling activities concerning of buyers and sellers. The foremost aims of communication system relating to marketing management is to raise the market opportunities market shares & levels of customers satisfaction.

Sources of Information as Required in Marketing Management

The communication system, as followed in marketing management, can collect and provide the informations related to this management are divided and briefly mentioned in two major parts as given here.

I. Market Research

i. Consumers' profile

ii. Demand analysis

iii. Demand forecast

Model - 7

SHOWING THE INFORMATION SYSTEM IN MARKETING MANAGEMENT

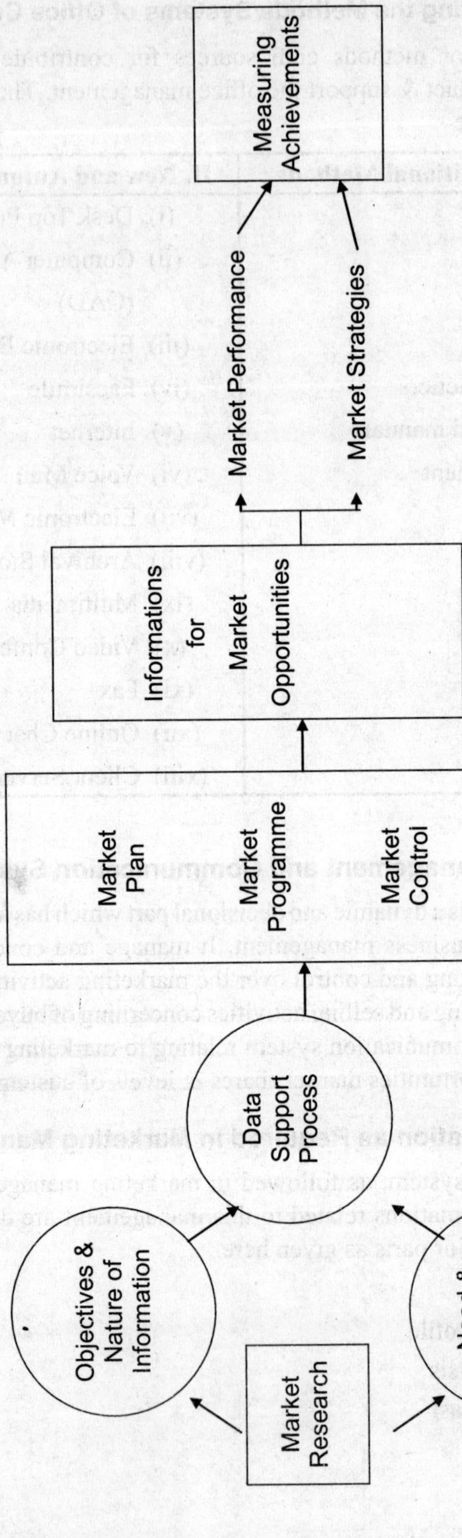

iv. Product research
v. Quality and brand research
vi. Sales volumes
vii. Price determination research
viii. Marketing cost
ix. Distribution cost

II. Promotion Mix

i. Analytical study of sales process
ii. Direct selling
iii. Advertising
iv. Sales promotion results
v. Publicity and public relations
vi. Value added aspects
vii. Relationship marketing

The model depicts that a communication network can be established right from the beginning to analyze and study the objectives need and nature of information required in this area. This is based on market research with the analytical process and evaluate the information and on the basis of these, the marketers can determine the market plan, market organize and devices of market control. The emerging part of market plan, market programme and market control also develop the information scenario and some foremost means of communication to cope up the market opportunities and worthwhile segments. Proper and amicable platform of opportunities might be able to create better strategies and performance in market segments. The strategies and performance mutually develop better achievements among the segmented area of market.

VIII. Accounting Management and Communication System

Accounting management is also an important part of functional management. It includes the systems, procedures, documents and records concerning the financial managerial and cost managements etc. It aims to manage and maintain the accounts, records, statements and other informative documents to use in these accounting area.

Communication System

In accounting management, the communication system is based on some documentations or data warehousing procedures. The data feedback is also an integrated part to develop the collection of data and sources of information which can be collected from different core areas of the accounting management.

Table 15: Showing the Sources of Informations in Accounting Management

Within the accounting management, there are three major core areas by which the informations can be occurred. The major areas of sources are given here:

(i) Concerning of Financial Accounting

(ii) Concerning of Management Accounting

(iii) Concerning of Cost Accounting

These areas are based on some means or methods by which the sources of informations can be developed. As such the methods communication system arising out of three areas for Accounting Management are given here

I. Concerning of Financial Accounting	II. Concerning of Management Accounting	III. Concerning of Cost Accounting
1. Income statement	1. Capital structure	1. Accounts receivable
2. Expenditure statement	2. Profit and loss statement	2. Accounts payable
3. Operating expenditures	3. Working capital structure	3. Components of cost
4. Profit and Loss A/c	4. Investment statements	4. Cost Analysis
5. Balance sheets	5. Current and fixed assets	
6. Investment statement	6. Cash flow statement	
7. Cash budgets	7. Fund flow statement	
8. Working capital structure	8. Cost structure	

IX. Service Management and Information System

In any business organization, the service management is also an important and feasible part which provide some assisting role towards achieving some betterment in product and services.

The information system contributing a lot of services in this management. This system provide some emerging issues for creating new avenues in services, social issues and professional values for improving the services etc.

The model depicts that the information system for services provide basically the need of emerging trends as finding out of the service sector. Within the role of MIS, the data processing is also an important part to elaborate the new aspects and values of services in any business organization. There are basically five areas of services like personal, professional, business, distribution and counseling etc. There are also some data warehousing mechanism to collect the needful informations for the availability and reliability of services in overall functional management. Basically the sources of informations for service management are social media & market research are commonly in our society. Besides, overall

Model-8

SHOWING THE INFORMATION SYSTEM FOR SERVICE MANAGEMENT

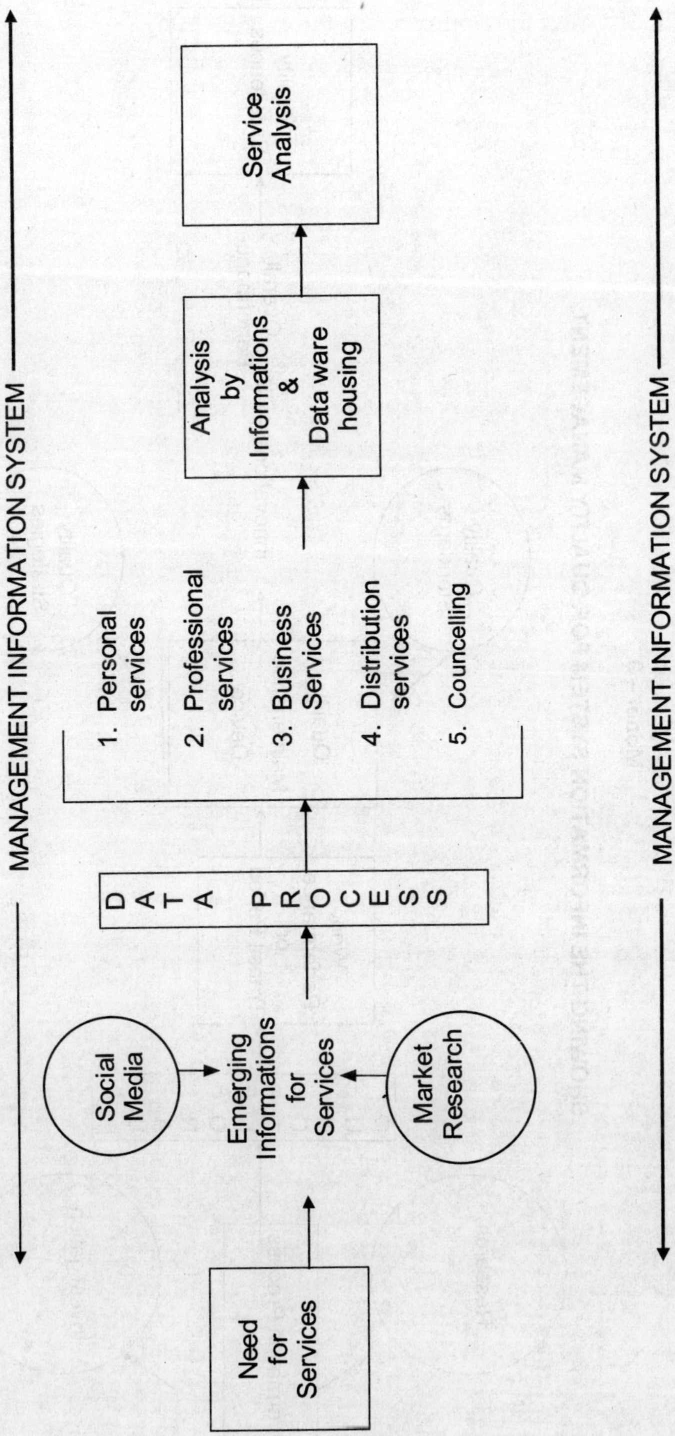

Model – 9

SHOWING THE INFORMATION SYSTEM FOR QUALITY MANAGEMENT

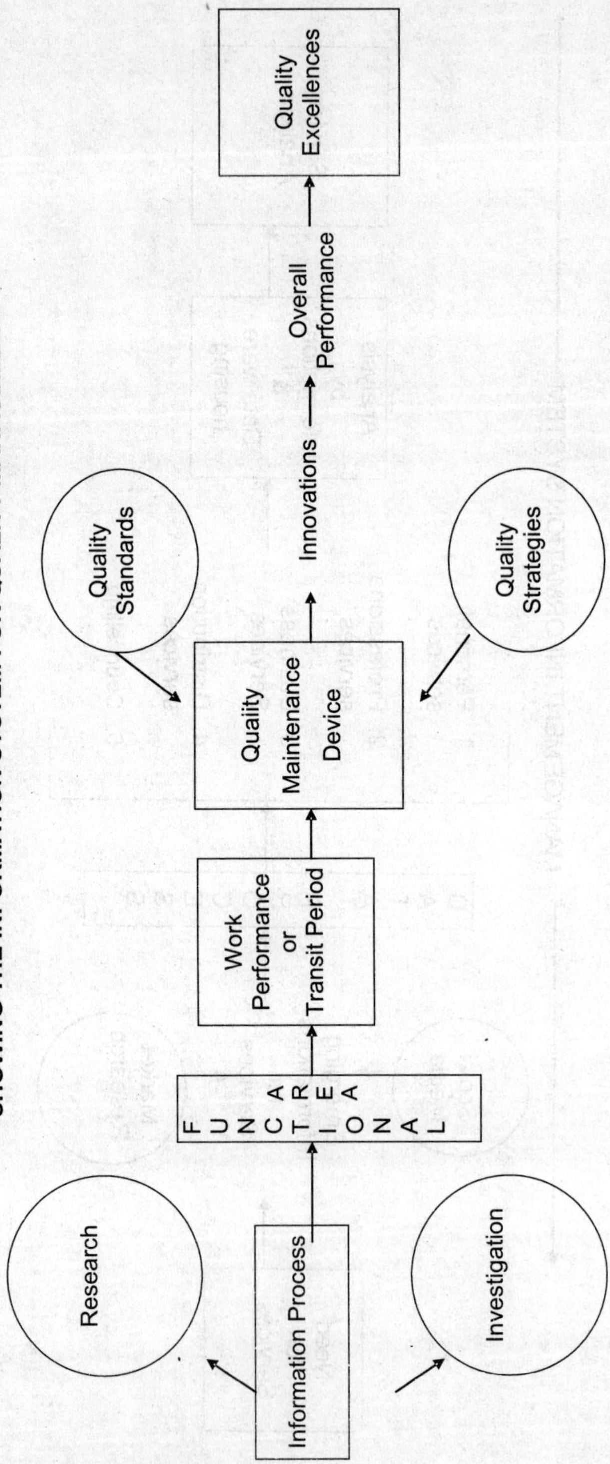

the means and media of communication in society are also directly or indirectly provide the essentialities of services in the field of business and management.

X. Total Quality Management and Communication System

Total quality is the notion that excellences are essential in all the functions of business and its allied activities. Quality management include the perspective and optimistic role to create and improve the quality of product and services as per predetermined goals and standards. The main tasks and contents of this management are briefly stated here as:

1. Implementation of the findings of product, market and service research.
2. To follow the acceptable norms and standards on the basis of target market & society at large.
3. To follow the means and parameters of the management of change.
4. To improve the quality of raw materials and other productive resources.
5. To improve the organizational structure and design.
6. To improve the techniques and means of performance management and evaluation in business.
7. To raise the levels of work performance with some innovations & perspective view points.

The overall quality management aims to develop the quality and better performance of the concern. Here, according to model no. 9 the research and investigation is the bases for making a plan to maintain quality of any product & services. In an organization, different quality maintenance devices are based on quality standards and quality strategies. With the applicability of these devices, the innovative measures are also developed to get an overall performance for quality excellences.

XI. Research and Development Management and Information System

Today it is needful to make some worthwhile coordination and follow the different aspects of changing environment. With the emerging issues like innovations, change environment, technological upgradation, professionalisation, social values, service patterns and new behavioural approaches, there is a need to manage the research, investigation and organize the developmental activities at large.

The model depicts the informative process to adopt the research and development activities in the business. Accordingly, the data support system & data analysis provide the feed back for new research SWOT analysis also develop a platform to accomodate the changing aspects.

As such, the different functional management needs to get concurrent services of communication system. It has studied that various models for these system are providing the means or transmitting the communication of different informations to functional management.

Model –10

SHOWING THE INFORMATION SYSTEM IN RESEARCH & DEVELOPMENT

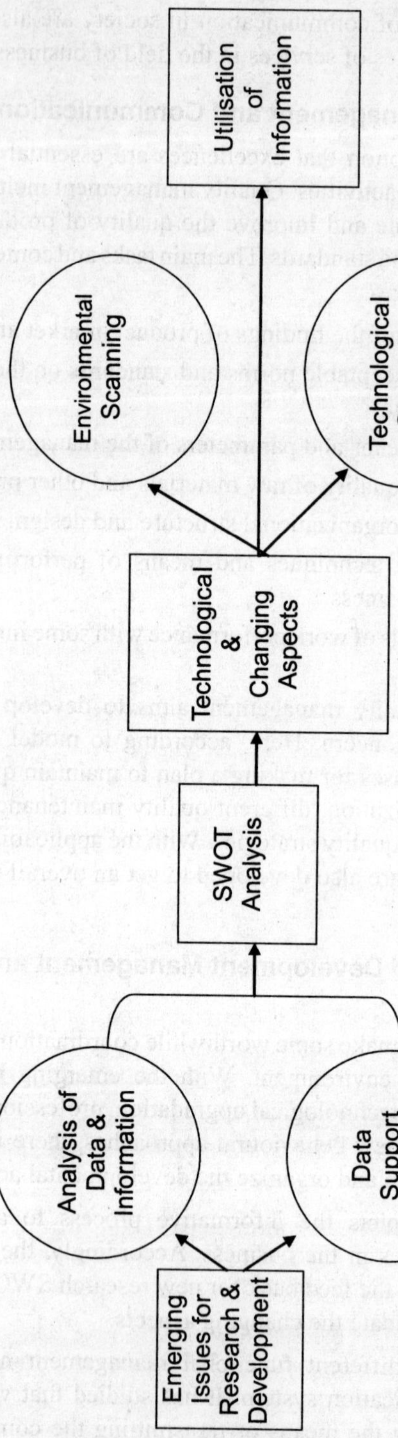

System Approaches

With the advent of new and innovative technologies, the formulation and performance of different functional area or departments are duly attached with new integrated approaches of system. A system is a group of interrelated components working together towards a common goal by accepting inputs and producing outputs through transformation process.

An efficient system have some major components like input, processing, feedback, environment, output and control etc.

Different Functional Areas – Based on System Analysis

Today every part of business has constituted by computerised process & the transforming is duly based on some systems approaches.

System approaches involve not only input output integrátion but some dynamic role of transforming process has also included in it.

The system analysis technologically based on different components that have provided various assistance to the functional area of business organization. It provide several emerging systems as briefly given here:

(i) Provide Input Process;

(ii) Feedback Storage;

(iii) Information Support System;

(iv) Manual Resources;

(v) Transactional Information Process;

(vi) Data Support System;

(vii) Research and Innovation.

Questions

(a) Short Questions

(i) Define Functional Management.

(ii) State two objectives of Functional Management.

(iii) Define Inventory/stock communication system.

(iv) Define the Cost communication system.

(v) Give the model of Personnel Communication System.

(vi) Describe in brief the information system of Marketing management.

(vii) Give the names of the Sources of information for Office Management.

(b) Descriptive Questions

(i) What is meant by Functional Management? What are the areas or components of functional management? Discuss in brief.

(ii) Define Functional Management. Describe the objectives and importance of Functional Management.

(iii) Describe the main functions of Production Management and also state the information system to be used in it.

(iv) Describe the information system to be used in 'Cost Management' and 'Quality Management'.

(v) What is meant by marketing management? Describe the information system to be used in it.

●●●

Part - V

Business / Management and Technological Bias

13 Chapter

Management Information System (MIS)

Within the purview of managerial phenomenon, the role and nature of different informations have an important and decisional part in transforming technique or system for creating and developing the information are included in Managerial Information System. It is simply a mechanism of computerization for the interest and benefits of managerial tasks and operating functions.

In any organization, informations are used for making and implementing different targets and policies for the achievement of organizational objectives. In fact, the interaction between 'individual' and 'group' is possible only through exchange of ideas and information which has a vital role in organization for survival as well as growth.

Definitions of MIS

The definitions of MIS are given here:

According to **Jerone Kanter** – "MIS is a system that aids management making, carrying out and controlling decisions."

According to **G.B. Davis** – "MIS as an integrated man/machine system for providing information to support the operations, management and decision making functions in organization."

Thus, MIS is a support system based on the concept and operating views to conduct and perform the organization functions.

Characteristics of MIS

The main characteristics of MIS are given here:

1. **Relevant Informations**

   MIS provide only relevant informations, though it is difficult to decide about relevancy. The information can be tested in terms of how it meets user requirement.
2. **Usefulness**

   It provides all the informations, which are useful, relevant and time tested.

3. **Required Format**

   All the informations provided in the required format which duly assists to management in decision making process.

4. **Quality Based**

   MIS is designed to Manage and organize the accuracy, appropriate, time tested and completeness of the required informations.

5. **Effective Transforming**

   MIS transforms various data into information in variety of ways according to the needs and requirements of the concern. There are many ways in which data are transformed within an information system.

6. **Integration**

   MIS develops the integration of all the system and sub-systems into a common and meaningful ventures. Computer network can be designed to facilitate data flow among these various systems.

7. **Opportunities**

   MIS enhances the needful informations in many ways by which the managers can find out the opportunities in anticipation.

8. **Computerized**

   Presently it is desirable to have a MIS system through computers. These have increased the effectiveness of the system.

9. **Comprehensiveness**

   MIS is comprehensive in nature. It includes the transforming and transaction process to include different aspects and level of management.

10. **Enhance Intelligences**

    MIS is based on the perspective platform of intelligences. It can develop new concept and ideologies for information support and allied activities.

11. **Coordinated**

    This system can develop the coordinated process to make a better feedback and utilizing area of informations. By and large the role of sub-system are also included in it.

12. **Sub-system**

    MIS is composed of all the sub-systems that are the part of the overall system. These sub-system share the goals of overall managerial missions and serve multilevel or multiple activities.

13. **Flexibility**

    MIS must be designed in such a manner that it can be easily modified. It must be capable of being easily expanded to accommodate new avenues of IT and of processing activities.

14. **Modularity**

    The MIS design is composed of many modules or sub-system with different processing aspects for making a better managerial performance.

Objectives of MIS

The objectives of management information system are as follows:

1. To provide and analyze different facts and informations to managers for their day to day work.
2. To provide effective means and base for performing the business tasks and avenues for accomplishing its objectives and goals.
3. To enhance the systems and technologies of operation research within the purview of operational management.
4. To provide and facilitate various resource based informations and to develop the processing, calculating and retrieval of data towards inducing MIS development.
5. To provide, analyze and evaluate the worthwhile informations to ascertain the decision making aspects and its processes.
6. To emphasis and develop the Decision Support System (DSS) with quantitative and non quantitative informations available to users.
7. To provide a better and strategically opportunities with some support system towards facing the challenges in business and in managerial functions.

MIS as well as Data Processing

A data processing system processes the transactions and produces reports. It represent the automation of routine processing to support operations. Since long it was performed manually or mechanically. The MIS is more comprehensive than data processing. It includes transaction processing to conduct managerial functions with decision models. Data processing involves the processing of data to make it more valuable and meaningful, thus transforming it into information. It includes a number of transactions and record maintenance in order to provide a data base for creating and providing informations to various users at the different level MIS is a wide area to make an overall system design which provide analysis and decision making supports. Data base is an essential part of routing transactions processing and reporting.

Infrastructure of Management Information System

The MIS is a planned, organized and procedural management system operating in a concern. It has the structural design consists of different infrastructural components which provide resource based role in it. As such, different infrastructures of MIS are given here:

1. **Manual Resources**

   The person who are involved to operate and follow the system, are a part of infrastructure. For effective working and proper maintenance, the manual resources like top managers and assistance are needful to make its infrastructure.

2. **Hardware**

   Within the framework of infrastructural design, the hardware also denotes the physical computer equipment and associated device. Broadly in the system of MIS, the hardware's can provide five basic functions *i.e.* input of data entry, output, secondary storage for data and programme, central processor and communication.

3. **Software**

   It is broad and dynamic work to include the directions, parameters of process work and programmes. It also direct the operation of the hardware. It can be divided mainly in two parts like system software and application software.

4. **Data Base**

   It denotes the processing work particularly of the collection and utilization of data. All data are used as per their utilization areas. The storage and filling process are also included in it.

5. **Procedure**

   The procedural structure is also an important part of MIS. It has different parts as data requirement, data collection, use instructions, direction for preparation of input, develop the output system and operating instructions etc.

6. **Environment**

   It has a wide aspect to include the conditions situations and internal and external factors of the concern to effect the working and operating of the system.

Elements/Components of Managerial Information System

There are three major elements or components of MIS i.e. Management, Information and System. They are important part to make some technological process to develop the analytical and implementing process in an organization.

I. Management

According to **Stanley Vance** – "Management is simply the process of decision making and control over the action of human being for the expressed purpose of attaining predetermined goals. **Henry Fayol** states that 'the manager is to forecast and to plan, to organize, to command, to coordinate and to control'. As such, management is basically a process of getting things done through and with people in formally organized groups. It involves allocation, utilization and mobilization of physical, human and other resources in an effective manner. **Peter F Drucker** noted and emphasize that the life of a manager is a perpetual decision making activity. Whatever a managers does, he does it through decision making. They transforms the resource based facts and figures into a productive and useful outputs.

Model – 11
SHOWING THE COMPONENTS OF MANAGEMENT INFORMATION SYSTEM (MIS)

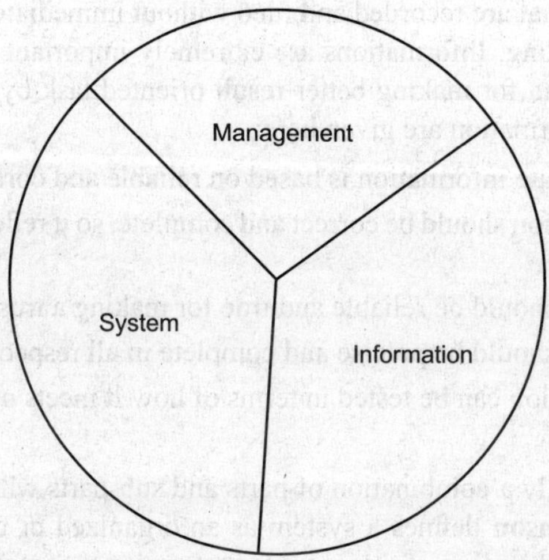

The model depicts three major components viz. Management, Information and System. They are composed in MIS.

Basic Features of Management

(i) Management is a continue process and in it every part or phase of managerial function is being perform in it;

(ii) The formulation of objectives is a basic criteria of existence for management because all organizations are deliberate and purposive creation;

(iii) Management is a system of planned and organized activities which involves a group of people involved in working towards a common objectives;

(iv) Management involved the people who are working and performing their tasks at different organization. Thus, management can integrates the role and behaviour of persons with the process of transmitting the informations;

(v) Decision making aspects also an important part in managerial rules. It basically involves to select the most appropriate alternatives. The quality of alternatives selected by managers determined the organizations performance. This process is duly based on the MIS programme.

The concept of implementing managerial task and performing decision making are being important part within the transforming process of data and informations.

II. Information

The information is a second constituent of MIS. According to **Davis and Olson** 'information is data that has been processed into a form that is meaningful to the recipient'. Informations are based on the raw form of data and symbols which represent actions, objects, quantities and events of the organization. Data is defined as groups of non-random symbols in the form of text, images or other form of voice actions. Data are facts and figures which usually take the form of historical records that are recorded and filed without immediate intention of using it for decision making. Informations are extremely important outcome based on resources based data for making better result oriented task by management. The basic points of information are given here:

(i) The appropriate information is based on reliable and correct data;

(ii) The information should be correct and complete, so it reflects the true picture of an issue;

(iii) Information should be reliable and true for making a trust;

(iv) Information should be precise and complete in all respect;

(v) The information can be tested in terms of how it meets user requirements.

III. System

A system is basically a combination of parts and sub-parts which are interrelated to each other. **Johnson** defines a system as an organized or complex whole; an assemblage or combination of things or parts forming a complex unitary whole.' The interrelationship among different parts may be set up as natural system or as man made systems. A system is not merely the totality of parts and sub-parts but their arrangement is more important. A system has following components:

(i) Input – It involves collecting and assembly the elements that enter the system for processing like raw materials, data, energy and human staff.

(ii) Processing – It involves transformation processes that convert input into output, like manufacturing process and data calculations.

(iii) Output – It involves transferring and result oriented elements that have been produced by the transformation process to their ultimate targets.

INTEGRATED APPROACHES

The components of MIS, mutually develops the interaction among them. Within it, receiving and evaluating feedback allows it to determine how well it is operating. In fact, the system as constitute the role of management, information and system that work together to process data and produce required information. It is utilized to support and perform managerial function and decision making.

STRUCTURAL FRAMEWORK OF MIS

MIS is more than a set of ideas or concepts and it is an operational system performing a variety of functions to produce outputs which are useful to the management of a concern. The MIS concept is now technically developed around a group of system, sub system and implemented as per overall plans. The system approaches are based on the computerized process and in fact the computer is only a tool of the MIS, not the MIS itself. With the help of system approaches the procedural framework can develop to transform the data into different goals based areas for developing the informations. It also provides to perform data processing operations to meet the informative requirements.

Model - 12

INTEGRATED ROLE OF MANAGEMENT INFORMATION SYSTEM (MIS)

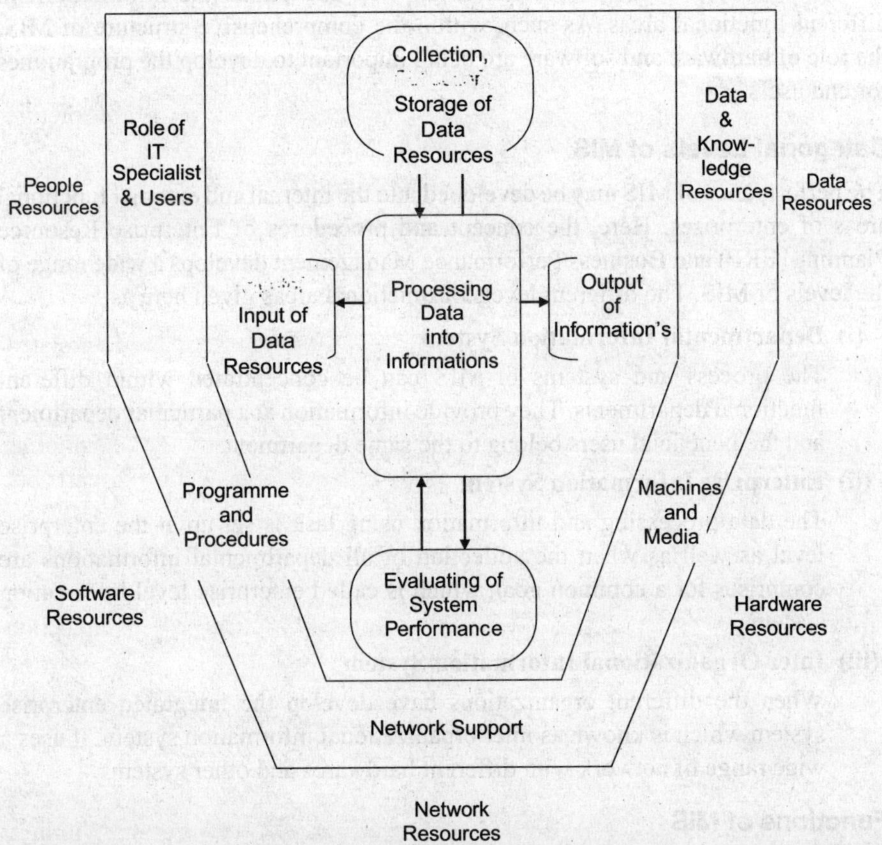

Here, the model pertaining the structural and integrated framework of MIS have broadly constitute the infrastructural components like manual resources, hardware, software, data base, procedures and environment etc. These components provides some supporting contribution to determine the means, standards and procedures for organizing and utilizing the basic components like management, information and system towards developing the objectives based informations. The model depicts that within the role of different components, the people have provided data and facts through their clients, designers and information system. A data base is a centrally controlled and integrated process for making logically organized data. Within the help of managerial cadres, the data can manage in order to be available for processing and have appropriatc quality and values. The hardware resources have the role of the devices of input of data entry, secondary storage for data and programmes and processor of storage and communication. Software system can develop the programmes and procedures.

Within the system performance, the informations can be evaluated and controlled according to the needs of the management. The network support system can contribute the software process to develop and utilize the informations in different functional areas. As such, within the comprehensive structure of MIS, the role of hardware and software are being important to develop the programmes for end users.

Categorial Levels of MIS

The performance of MIS may be developed into the internal and external functional areas of enterprises. Here, the concept and procedures of Enterprise Resource Planning (ERP) and Business Performance Management develops a wide range of the levels of MIS. The different levels of functional areas given here as:

(i) Departmental Information System

The process and systems of MIS can be concentrated within different functional departments. They provide information at a particular department and the beneficial users belong to the same department.

(ii) Enterprise Information System

The data processing and information using task is set up at the enterprise level as well as when the collection of all departmental informations are comprises for a common goal, which is called enterprise level information system.

(iii) Inter Organizational Information System

When the different organizations have develop the integrated enterprise system which is known as inter organizational information system. It uses a wide range of network with different hardwares and other systems.

Functions of MIS

MIS is a dynamic programme to combine the role of processing to provide informations and the systems of computers. The major functions of MIS are given here:

(i) Collecting of Data

Basically the role of MIS is to determine the information as required for functional areas of management. At operational level the data base system is collected and stored, which can be collected from internal or external sources.

(ii) Stores Data

Within the development of database it is stored at hard disk and it may be classified and loaded by different files into computers.

(iii) Data Processing

With the requirement of users, the data can be processed and transformed into information in various of ways.

(iv) Develop Sub-system

MIS can develop the sub-system that are the part of the overall system. These systems involved and incorporate the process of achieving managerial goals on the basis of their multiple and multilevel activities.

(v) Provide Feedback

MIS may provide feedback about its own performance and effectiveness. Here, the processing errors might be able to diagnose the problem and making a feedback records for managers.

(vi) Provide Informations to Managers

With the help of storing, collecting and processing data, the important function is to provide needful informations to managers for their use.

(vii) Develop Different Levels

MIS can develop their information at different level of management. At top level, it provide strategical information, at middle level, to provide tactical information and at the lower level, it provide operational information for smooth conducting the organizational tasks.

MIS Promotes Information Technologies

The concept and systems of MIS can promote the I.T. in different ways. The promotional role of MIS are given here:

(i) Multiple Information

The computer system provide multiple type of informations accurately. The managers or decision makers can carry out a thorough analysis of the problem and get it proper way for optimum decisions.

(ii) Composition of Systems

MIS might be able to develop the composition of the role of different systems and sub-systems. The coordination among the systems may be helpful in utilizing the informations.

(iii) Speedly Processed

Within the competitive and complex business environment, the computers are able to develop their processing task very speedly. By quick speed, MIS may be worthwhile for the enterprise.

(iv) Optimum Decision

MIS programme can be helpful to managers for better and appropriate decisions at the enterprise level.

(v) Continuous Process

MIS is a continuous process. The integrated and creative process of MIS may be able for managers to guide, supervise, motivate and control the subordinates continuously.

(vi) Intellectual Process

MIS is an intellectual and rational process to develop some useful, intellectual views and concepts through reformation of data and feedbacks.

(vii) Effectiveness of Informations

MIS may develop and made available the qualitatively information. Here, it is quite easy to provide timely, accurate and desired informations for the purpose of decision making.

Limitations of MIS

(i) MIS is not so useful for making non programmed decisions;

(ii) MIS is not able to provide information suitable for every nature and types for decisions;

(iii) MIS is not substitute for effective management. It is merely a tool to assists in making decisions at different managerial levels.

(iv) In fact probably MIS output is based on the quality and availability of input data.

(v) MIS system may not have success with the fast and growing changing environment.

Other Technologies

Within the computer based new technologies the MIS is an important part and besides it, there are several other technologies applicable to support the communication process. A brief and theoretical focus is given here to emphasize the new and other technologies as under:

(i) Artificial Intelligence

It is a branch of computer science to study how to make new ideas and concepts at which people are better at the moment. It is a mindset a way of looking at and solving problems from a specific point of views. It is a system that can generate computer software to perform symbolic integration and develops the learning aspects.

Artificial intelligencies can be able to make proper work mindsets. It is helpful to management through the means as given here:

(a) An understanding process can develop by visual images;

(b) Informations are available to determine the policies and plans;

(c) It is helpful to evaluate and analyze the situation and handle them properly;

(d) To solve the problems by reasonable and justified causes;

(e) The perspective and creative approaches may be developed.

(ii) Enterprise Resources Planning (ERP)

It is an integrated system that manage and organize business practices associated with the operation and production aspects of a concern. It is the technological ground of e-business, an enterprise wide transaction framework with the integrated approaches of different functional departments and processes. It includes the system of multifacility, data base creation and electronic data interchange etc. It is helpful to get needful informations, reports, performance and control of the different segments of the concern. It develops the integrated functional design to make coordinated control of the entire organization. The ERP model may also be helpful in formation of planning, decision supports, inventory design, material control, accounting control and overall organizational functions.

(iii) Executive Information System (E.I.S.)

It is just similar of MIS and intended to facilitate and support the information particularly at critical and complex environment. This system is going on with the process and structure of MIS. It is designed to support higher level decision making process. It provide more detailed and intensive informations with a variety of sources. It may support in different areas like implementing the strategic planning, to analyze the strength and weaknesses of concern to project new product lines, to develop new market segments, to acquisition of new equipments, to make effective resources allocation etc. It includes the components like input data entry device, central processing unit, data base, text base software and graphic base etc.

(iv) Multimedia

It is a technology involved a variety of media including audio, video, text, graphics and animation separately or in combination using computer to communicate 'ideas or informations'. The technology of multimedia has provided several assistance to management as under:

(a) It is helpful to present the policies, plans and programmes to organization;

(b) It is helpful towards project presentation at meetings;

(c) It is helpful in tele-conferencing;

(d) It can organize network meeting;

(e) It can manage and organize the training programme;

(f) It can develop new and interactive softwares.

(v) Decision Support System (D.S.S.)

Decision Support System (D.S.S.) is emphasized on support and it allows the decision maker to retrieve data and test alternative solutions during the process of problem solving. It is an interactive, specialized data base and analytical model system to support to solve the unstructured problems. It support all aspects and phases of decision making. It includes hardware resource, software resource, data resource, model resource, system packages as provided by consulting organizations.

(vi) Role of Chief Information Officer (C.I.O.)

The CIO is a part of senior executives and have most leading capacity particularly for managing and monitoring the information procedures. I leads all usage of I.T. from a business perspectives. He is responsible to develop a working relationship between I.T. and business units, that has applicable for better work performance. He manage and organize the entire I.T. framework for proper availability and performance of the means and medias of communication. He can redefine the required skill and abilities of employees for conducting the I.T. structure at the organization.

MIS in Indian Scenario

The rapid advancement of technology and consequent advent of computer science have emerged a new and innovative way particularly in communication scenario. In our country after 1950, the advent of computers have developed the operation of MIS in few and selected areas. The major hurdles are the reluctance on the part of higher management to convince themselves of the usefulness of MIS. With their old and traditional views they do not support to follow the system of MIS. Besides there is a lack of proper training and there are ineffective handling, semantic barriers, status problems and inadequate attention have been mainly responsible for the slow development of computerized MIS.

Questions

(a) Short Questions

(i) Define MIS.

(ii) Give any two characteristics of MIS.

(iii) Give any two objectives of MIS.

(iv) What are the components of MIS?

(v) Define 'Software'.

(vi) What is meant by 'System'?

(vii) What is multiple informations?

(viii) What are the infrastructural components of MIS?

(b) Descriptive Questions

(i) What is meant by 'Management Information System'? Describe the major elements of MIS.

(ii) What are the objectives of MIS? Describe the advantages and disadvantages of MIS.

(iii) Describe the MIS. Also state the structural framework of MIS.

(iv) How the MIS promotes the I.T. sector? Discuss.

●●●

14 Chapter

Internet

The internet is an alarming and revolutionary status within the field of information technology. It is a network that can be as simple as linking two computers or may consist of millions of different types of computers and peripherals, connected directly or indirectly. It is a huge network of computers and servers. It is called a worldwide computer network to which different computers are connected. As such, it denotes a data communication system that is made up of hardware and softwares. Generally, a computer network may includes physical infrastructural parts like cables, wires, fiber optic lines, under sea cables and satellites etc. As such it can be called 'Network of Network'.

CHARACTERISTICS OF INTERNET

The basic characteristics of Internet are given here:

(i) It is a decentralized system in that a large number of individual computers are connected all over the world;

(ii) A huge number of people with wide area use the internet;

(iii) The internet web page is basic and important text file by which informations can be viewed on internet;

(iv) It is composed of millions of files pertaining to thousands of subjects, matters, disciplines and professionals;

(v) It can be cumbersome and confusing if it is not perform properly with some required technological guidelines;

(vi) It provides a large share of software tools and systems as well as their perspective utilities;

(vii) Some of the important and considerable protocols as file transfer protocol, hyper text transfer protocols and main transfer protocols are being used in internet.

HISTORICAL BACKGROUND

The internet was initially emerged in 1969 in USA as a small network of four areas located at the four universities viz SRI, UCLA, UCSB and university of Utah to facilitate sharing of scientific data and computing resources between these remote sites. This network was jointly built by the concerns as The Network Work Grouping and Other named Bolt-Beranek and Newman (BEM) in Cambridge. During 1980, both the concerns developed the additional network to connect with another organization.

APPLICATION AREA OF THE INTERNET

The internet has a wide area for its utilization. The areas are as given here:

(i) Online Communication

The electronic mail service is extensively used today by computer users around the world to communicate with each other. With this facility, the internet has proved to be a rapid and productive communication tool for millions of users.

(ii) Product Promotion

Several commercial organizations are effectively using the internet services for promoting their products. These organizations make use of Gopher, or WWW server sites focused on disseminating timely information about corporate situation, product knowledge, recent strategic alliances, press releases, and other information of potential interest to existing and prospective customers.

(iii) Exchange of Views on Topics of Common Interest

The internet has a number of news groups of users to exchange their views concepts and personalities on some topic of common interest.

(iv) Customer Support Service

Many software organizations are also using the internet to provide unprecedented levels of timely customer support. The combined electronic mail, FTP, and other services on the internet provide all the enabling tools necessary to provide such first-rate customer support.

(v) Software Sharing

The internet provides access to a large number of shareware software development tools and utilities. A few examples of such available shareware tools are compilers, code libraries, mail servers, and operating systems.

(vi) Posting of Information of General Interest

The internet is also being extensively used as a large electronic bulletin board on which information of general interest can be posted to bring it to the attention of interested users around the world. Some commonly posted information includes career opportunities, conference and event announcements, and calls for papers for conference and journals.

(vii) On-line Shopping

The internet has also facilitated the introduction of a new market concept that consist as virtual shops. These shops remain open 24 hours all the year round and are accessible to purchasers all around the world. They provide information about products or services for sale through FTP, Gopher, or WWW servers. Using the internet services, customers submit specific product queries and request specific sales quotes.

(viii) On-line Journals and Magazines

The internet now has literally thousands of electronic subscriptions that can be found both free as well as low cost. There are many useful sites on the internet that deal with electronic versions of many journals and magazines. For example, the internet edition of the Jagran newspaper is available at the internet site http://www.jagran.com. Researchers are working in the direction to extend this idea to support full-fledged electronic libraries on the internet.

(ix) Feedback About Products

In addition to product promotion, commercial organization are also using the internet to gather information about user satisfaction of exiting products, market opportunities of new products, and ideas for potential new products. This is usually accomplished by putting up an interactive survey application by the organization on a WWW or Gopher site on the internet.

(x) Worldwide Video Conferencing

Worldwide video conferencing is an emerging service on the internet that allows a group of users located around the globe to talk and interact with each other as if they were sitting and discussing in a single room. The parties interacting can see each other talking on their computer screens and can hear each other's voice through a special audio-device fixed in their computers.

Working of Internet

The internet working is based on the services of integrated digital network, which provides a wide area of transmission of data. It involves a number of steps that are essential to develop the main task. Firstly, it is required to locate an Internet Service Provider (ISP) for a particular area. Typically, our local ISP will offer you a monthly package which will include; email and web access, download/ upload capabilities and newsgroups. If these terms don't seem familiar to us, do not concerned. If the process of ISP allows us to continue then the user can get an ISP and signed their service agreement, next we will need to install some software on computer. In many cases your ISP will help us with that installation. Below is a list of the software that we should install on our computers.

- Telecommunications Software, including Winsock, or other Internet protocol transceiver software.
- A World Wide Web Browser.
- An E-mail program
- An FTP program

When all these software installed, we will be ready to access the Internet. Once we are ready, it's now time to connect to the Internet. How is it accomplished?

Well it's simple really, our computer will dial a local number, which is provided by your ISP. Once you have logged into your ISP, we are connected to the Internet.

Internet Methods and Services

Within the dynamic process and multidynamic techniques of Internet, the methods or tools and services, that also shows their components and processes to use in. The methods and services are briefly mentioned here:

I. *Information Retrieval Methods*

(i) File transfer protocol
(ii) Client server relations
(iii) Personal/user I.D.
(iv) Use gopher server
(v) Transformation of data and information from one computer to the other.

II. *Clients and Servers*

(i) Client PCs
(ii) Develop and maintain intermittent connections
(iii) Maintain and control the flow of information from one place to other.

III. *Bandwidth*

(i) Maintain and control speed of internet connectivity
(ii) Develop Data-handling capacity
(iii) Regularize to control speed of transfering the data

IV. *Internet Connectivity*

(i) Dial-up modem connections
(ii) ISDN connection
(iii) DSL and Coaxial connections

V. *Multi Media Information Tools*

(i) Home page
(ii) World Wide Web (WWW)

VI. *Internet Services*

(i) Electronic mail
(ii) Telnet process
(iii) File transfer protocol
(iv) Chatting and Instant messages
(v) Internet telephony
(vi) Video conferencing
(vii) Mailing list
(viii) Web browser

Advantages of Internet

(i) It is available to common man and it has brought the world closer, as well as it is available at every part of society;

(ii) It offer online communication facility that is a two way communication among different persons;

(iii) It represent the medias in the form of letters, telegrams, circulars and fax etc.;

(iv) It sort out business functions like ordering of items, making quotations, payment bills, exchange of documents can be carried out on the internet;

(v) Electronic mail transmitting process can be performed in a short time that save time and energy;

(vi) The servers around the world are constantly transmitting the information available round the clock;

(vii) The interest provide easily the different and relevant informations on almost all the subject at a time;

(viii) It does not discriminate among different users belongs to different groups or occupation or any society;

(ix) It reduce undesirable cost and expenditures particularly of printing and stationary;

(x) It may develop and improve the manual performance at every step.

Disadvantages of Internet

(i) The internet may distribute undesirable, unreliable and unchecked informations;

(ii) It may develop isolate and separate people as they may spend a long time on internet instead of personal contact;

(iii) It reduce the face to face contact among people and thereby the personal recognition and identification has becomes meaningless;

(iv) It may develop fraud and mischieves;

(v) It may enable piracy and sabotages;

(vi) Sometime, it may not be able to provide an entire contents or subject matter as required by users;

(vii) It may also carry uncontrolled and unrestricted pornography.

As such, Internet provides a variety of services particularly of a wide linking of computers with each other, online business transactions, cash payments and transfers, locating sites, video conferencing and different online services etc.

Questions

(a) Short Questions

(i) What do you mean by Internet?

(ii) State any four advantages of Internet.

(iii) State any four disadvantages of Internet.

(iv) State any two applicable areas of Internet.

(v) State any two characteristics of Internet.

(b) Descriptive Questions

(i) Define Internet.

(ii) State the advantages and disadvantages of Internet.

(iii) Describe the applicable areas of Internet.

(iv) Briefly describe different Internet methods and services.

●●●

15 Chapter

e-Commerce

E-commerce or electronic commerce is a similar concept of e-business. It is general concept which covers any form of business transactions or exchanging the information. It may include buying, selling, negotiation, payment and different steps for transactions in business as a whole to perform over computer networks.

E-commerce is carrying out of network of business activities that lead to an exchange of value across telecommunicative network. It is a new application of advanced information technology to increase the effectiveness of commercial practices among partners. It is about using the power of digital information to know the need and preference of every customer and to customize products and services for them and then to deliver them as quickly as possible. Now e-commerce invariably uses the world wide web at some focal point in the transactional way to encompass a wider range of technologies like e-mail as well.

OBJECTIVE OF e-COMMERCE

(i) To develop speedily the communication contacts between buyers and sellers;

(ii) To perform different commercial tasks as laid down in business transactions;

(iii) To create and develop the power of digital information to know the profile of customers for effective customization;

(iv) To improve or to re-engineer the business processes to maximize the benefits and quality of electronic commerce;

(v) To develop better quality of products and services as required by customers.

The model depict the defining concept of e-commerce by four different views. The concept of e-commerce may be defined in the form of online perspective processing, communication perspectives, service perspectives and business process perspectives.

Model – 13

SHOWING THE AREA OF DEFINING e-COMMERCE

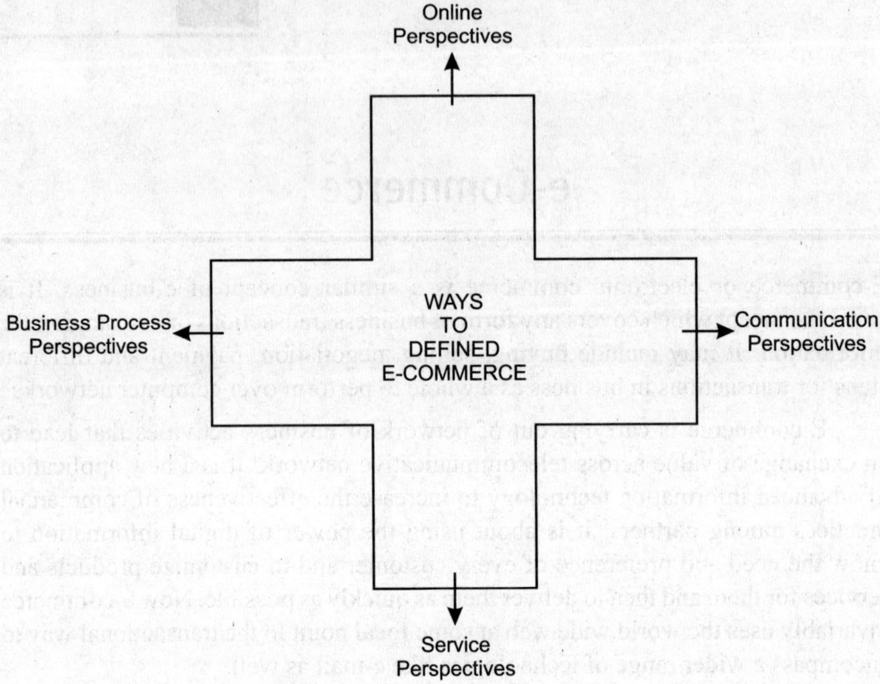

ASPECTS IN IMPLEMENTING e-COMMERCE

There are some important aspects to be considered for implementing the technology of e-commerce. Basically they must be considered while performing the e-commerce process. The aspects are as under:

(i) Value

Every buyer and seller wants to know that they should get their return out of their products and price. The auto-transmission, business process automation, optimum return and minimizing the cost etc. must be involved in this process. The systems used to develop these systems are needful aspects in e-commerce.

(ii) Cost

The concept of e-commerce requires some signifying investment and returns in new and innovative techniques as applicable in core business areas. This system also requires some worthwhile investment in software, hardware, manual resources and transmitting process. The cost-minimizing efforts should be developed at every part of it.

(iii) Productivity Gains

It is required to develop the digital products more qualitatively and have better productivity. The products should be improved with the informations about customers' tastes and preferences within e-commerce transactions.

(iv) Interoperability

Within the process as managed in e-commerce, the exchange of documents without manual intervention must be helpful in cost and time savings, improved performance and develops more value chains.

(v) Team Work

It requires to develop the coordination and team spirit for work together. By mailing transactions the people collaborately exchange informations and develop the interaction with different partners.

BASIC INFRASTRUCTURE IN e-COMMERCE

The basic infrastructure as involved in the system and process of e-commerce are given here:

(i) A wide range of multimedia contents are required in it. These are resources based aspects to perform the process of e-commerce.

(ii) Large database with some appropriate data storages are its essential part.

(iii) Session Initiation Protocol (SIP) are providing desired services for the user as point to point calls, multipoints conferencing, text, audio and video etc. SIP enables the initiation of an interactive experience involving multimedia elements as video, voice, chat, gaming and virtual reality.

(iv) Web Servers also handle the customers' orders, calculate the customers' orders, computing taxes and displays the details of customers.

(v) On line informediaries are also some popular web site that provide specialized informations on behalf of manufacturers and their potential customers.

TYPES OF e-COMMERCE

The e-commerce can be categorized in various parts as under:

I. B2B (Business to Business)

B2B is an important part in marketing communication in that a business house contact to another business for promoting the business performance specifically for competitive advantages, enhancing campaign plan, establishing positioning collateral sales supports, quality maintenance, advertising and public relations etc.

II. B2C (Business to Consumer)

Within e-commerce, B2C is a popular and most decisional category for selling physical goods or services directly to the end-customers. It is consumer oriented application that develop the market with new strategies to grab the share in the global market. There are few models as emerged through web sites as given here:

(i) Online intermediatories to provide specialized information about product and services;

(ii) Community informations to make interaction with different customers;

(iii) Advertising based informations, which develop a web site to provide advertising services on premium or admissible charges.

III. C2B (Consumer to Business)

Consumer to Business is a growing model in that consumer can make contact with their business unit to inform about grievances, problems, complaints as well as their requirement about product and services. The consumers can get different day to day services through web sites of C2B.

IV. C2C (Consumers to Customers)

C2C sites are usually provide the consultation and auction services among consumers. They briefly consult themselves and also contact business houses to get some ways and means of transactions. Precisely, these sites provide connections with not only among consumers but with business houses also. It is easy to use web browser for all types of hardware combinations and operating system.

Model – 14

SHOWING THE e-COMMERCE PROCESS

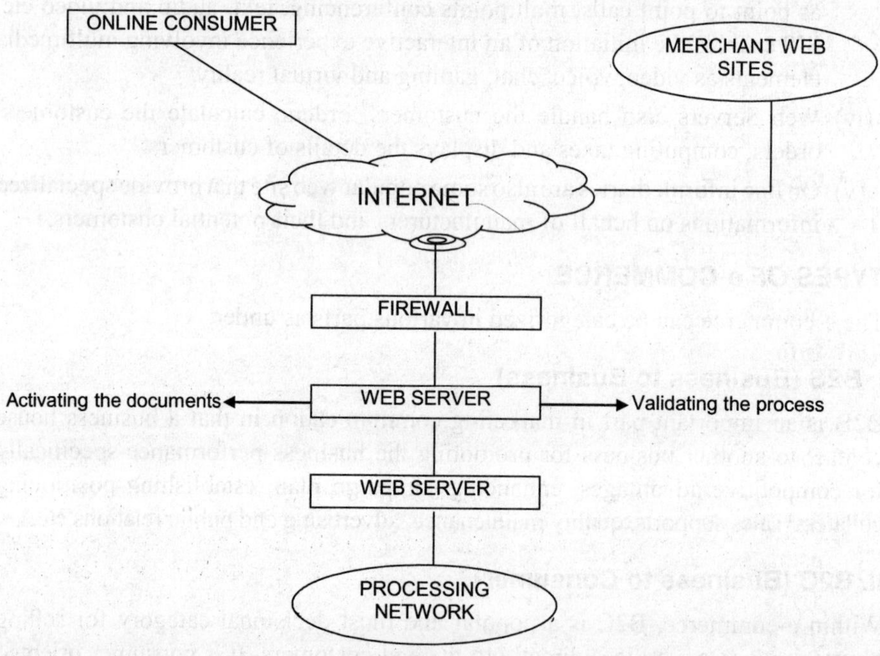

The model no. 14 depicts in shorter form about the procedural framework of e- commerce.

PROCEDURAL FUNCTIONING OF e-COMMERCE

The functioning of e-commerce process is briefly given here. Initially the customer can log into the internet using a desired web browser to connect the another party's website. The fire well system protect the unauthorized users and disconnect the disturbed events through the sites. The customers can browse to find out the products available on the site and select items to buy and point out items in the electronic equivalent by shopping cart. After that the vouchers, bills and other documents are being transferred from one party to the other. The shipping and unloading address are also mutually transferred to each other. Here, the payment information, calculations, credit card number and code number, place of Bank unit and other things also included in transforming process. Web server also provide different opportunities and directions to perform the trading transactions among the buyer and sellers.

Applications of e-commerce

Within a wide area of internet, the sphere of e-commerce is one part to make trading and commercial transactions. The area in that e-commerce may be applicable are given here:

(i) Electronic Data Interchange (EDI)

It is the system to interlink the data and information among different computer systems. It is used by business houses based on channel design that makes a large number of regular transactions. It use standardized coding system which is extensively used for channelizing the business transactions.

(ii) Electronic Market

Internet and e-commerce technologies develop a number of trade segments through EDI and CAD systems as applicable in e-commerce. They can develop regular and standardized transactions among trading parties. E-commerce includes the technologies that can be used to advertise and make once of sales of a wide range of goods and services. It is governed and managed by the commercial use of the internet.

(iii) Information Sharing

E-commerce also develops the information sharing process which shows awareness of product and services among customers. This can be in the form of marketing and advertising. It can also mean providing information to prospective customers about the products or services in various forms, to help them in their information gathering process. This can be easily achieved using the internet. The means and media that can be helpful are given here:

(i) Online communities

(ii) Chat rooms

(iii) Multi-party conferences

(iv) Bulletin board systems

(v) News groups.

The internet allows business houses to set up extensive customer support features. For instance, the customers can send their queries or report problems using the internet, which can be directed to the appropriate help desk staff for resolutions.

(iv) Electronic Banking

The increase in penetration of personal computers there are several financial management software packages such as Quicken and Microsoft Money have emerged. The user can later use the software to balance the checkbook, summarize credit card purchases, track stocks and other investments. Personal finance management through these software packages requires duplication of efforts, *i.e.*, once by the financial institution and once by the user.

With the wide availability and access of the internet, electronic banking empower consumers to access their accountants, carry out transactions through web browsers or web enabled personal software packages. Customers can view account details, transfer funds, pay bills, order checks, and review account history.

(v) Electronic Searching

The emergence of the internet and e-commerce technologies have been developing the tasks by putting the information for mass number of people. Here, telephone directories listing personal phone numbers and business phone numbers play an important role in locating the person or business as the case may be. The listing of business phone numbers is often organized by business classifications to assist in locating a business for a particular function. Many a times phone companies assist by permitting.

(vi) Education and Learning

Internet has lately been used as a delivery vehicle for training and learning as well. The web technology provides a uniform delivery mechanism for textual, multimedia, and animated contents. E-learning has already taken powerful roots and is emerging most predominantly in the information technology universe, presumable, because IT professionals are more conformable working with the new technology and have access to high speed internet connections for the fast transmission required for media rich lessons.

(vii) Internal Business Systems

Some of the applicable areas as performed within the process of internet and e-commerce are Customer Relation Management (CRM), Enterprise Resources Planning (ERP), Human Resources Management (HRM), Content Management System (CMS) and different aspects of Digital process etc.

(viii) Electronic Payment

The electronic payment process, presents a vital and complex challenge to business and financial institutions to develop efficient, flexible, and secure payment systems for electronic commerce. A variety of payment systems have evolved for electronic fund transfers, including several major ways to provide security for transactions and payments over the internet.

Electronic payments are the central part of e-commerce activities as it deals with the strategies for the payment of goods and services by online customers. An electronic payment also refers to the activity of account settlement where the prompt settlement of payments is crucial. Here, the conventional instruments for payments such as demand draft, credit notes, cheque are not suited to e-commerce.

Various instruments, which may be used to make payments on the internet are Credit/Debit cards. Smart cards, Electronic Cash, Electronic Wallet, etc. Important issues related to the Electronic payment systems include the methods, form and characteristic of payment instrument such as e-cash, credit/debit cards, how to minimize the financial risk such as leakage of information, mistakes and frauds and finally devising methods for the completion of electronic payment cycle.

(ix) E-Business Models

The different e-business models, as applicable to promote the product, service and information flows. These are directly or indirectly linked within the process of e-commerce. The most adopted models are as online shopping, e-malls, e-auctions, value chain services, e-procurement and voice mails etc.

Advantages of e-commerce

(i) A closer relationship can be developed amongst business sellers whose customer base is on the internet;

(ii) E-commerce can improve information sharing among different partners of business and promote the delivery services well on time;

(iii) E-commerce create knowledge market. Customers' knowledge can be enhanced on topics such as news about local events, market research, industrial report, software etc. that can be distributed easily over the other sources;

(iv) It allows more business partners to interact and develop their mutual interest;

(v) Business organizations selling their goods through catalogues can reach additional global customers at lower costs;

(vi) Companies dealing in digital assets such as inventory information, logos, image libraries etc. can sell their products electronically;

(vii) For wholesalers, distributors, retailers etc., it is convenient and efficient to buy from web sites;

(viii) High quality, specialized products can be easily available on internet by the retailers;

(ix) For items subjected to frequent changes, e.g., shares and bonds etc., the changes in rates/quotations can be known and analyze instantly;

(x) Organizations can conduct interviews and personal contact through internet to select suitable candidates for their requirements;

(xi) Group discussion can be conducted for corporate office, industrial houses, business firms, universities, etc.;

(xii) Well established companies can establish their subsidiary sites for ancillaries, related products etc. on their corporate website;

(xiii) More customization is possible in providing different services;

(xiv) It helps people to work together. It can develop the platform to exchange information and work on solutions.

Disadvantages of e-commerce

(i) There is a continuing shortage of e-literate people at working place. Only few persons have e-commerce skills, internet experience and advance computer knowledge;

(ii) There is lack of reliabilities, security and some communication protocols;

(iii) The software technologies are not so developed with changing situations;

(iv) There is some technical problem to integrate the internet and e-commerce software with some applications;

(v) The cost of developing the software of e-commerce is very high;

(vi) There is lack of the sources of finding some new opportunities that are useful for customers' satisfaction;

(vii) Many legal issues are as yet not cleared and not refined enough for many transactions;

(viii) There is lack of proper and wide feedback about knowing and learning the systems and applications of e-commerce.

As such, a fundamental and basic concept and working of e-commerce has discussed as an important part of Business Communication.

Questions

(a) Short Questions

(i) Define e-commerce.

(ii) Define Electronic Market.

(iii) Define B2B and B2C.

(iv) Define Electronic Banking.

(v) What are the various aspects in implementing e-commerce?

(vi) What is Electronic Payment?

(vii) State any four names for application of e-commerce.

(viii) State any four advantages of e-commerce.

(b) Descriptive Questions

(i) What is e-commerce? What are the basic aspects for performing the e-commerce?

(ii) Describe the advantages and disadvantages of e-commerce.

(iii) Describe the advantages of e-commerce. What basic infrastructure is required for implementation of e-commerce?

(iv) What are the different categories in e-commerce?

(v) State the structural process/design for e-commerce.

(vi) What are the applicable areas of e-commerce? Briefly describe them.

●●●

Part - VI

Barriers and Perspective Effectiveness of Communication

16 Chapter

Barriers of Communication

In any business, the communication itself a decisional and dynamic part to manage and organize different tasks, although a major role and assistance of communication are at least partially successful and some of them are perfect and few are imperfect with the reasons of appropriate causes. In fact, the communication barriers and obstacles are more or less having an inevitable part of the entire business organization. The barriers are mostly related with languages, poor communication skill, negligence, behavioural aspects, transmitting problems, organizational structure and differences in different demographical factors. Broadly, the communication barriers can be classified into five major parts as given here:

Types of Communication Barriers
- (i) Physical barriers
- (ii) Semantic barriers
- (iii) Psychological barriers
- (iv) Organizational barriers
- (v) Cross cultural barriers

I. Physical Barriers

The physical barriers are related to the system, persons and physical viability of the resources, some of the physical barriers are given here:

(i) Sources

The sources from which the message originates is very important. If the receiver or sender have some indifferent or biased attitude and they have some hostile feelings then the sources are neither trustworthy nor acceptable by the partners.

(ii) Distance

Due to a long distance the partners are not able to make face to face interaction and not hear properly to make worthy relations.

(iii) Source of communication

If the receivers dislike the source or harbors any prejudice against him, he will automatically not listen to the sender. If the source of communication is unreliable, unjustified and dislikes then the source of communication becomes on hurdle.

(iv) Time

If message get delayed they become redundant and useless. They also create confusion. Communication is useful and effective only if it is conveyed at the right time and to the right person.

(v) Physical Noise

Physical noise which creates disturbances in the environment can be a barrier in the communication process. Both the sender and the receiver can be hampered by it. Messages become distorted and also inaudible because of the surrounding noise. For example, when the TV set is on, at a high volume, it becomes difficult to follow a conversation in the same room.

(vi) Defects in the Medium

There may be a defect in the communication device, which are being used. For example, during a speech to large audience, the microphone does not work properly so the effect of the speech is minimized or may be poor. A partial failure of the mechanical equipment is more dangerous than a complete failure, because a partial failure carries an incomplete or distorted message, which may cause a wrong action to be taken.

(vii) State of Health

A poor physical condition can affect any persons' efficiency in all working areas. This illness or any ailments can come in the way of speaking and listening.

II. Semantic Barriers

These are to do with the language. It is not very easy to do away with these barriers.

(i) Most of the messages are badly expressed. Often they are vague and not clear. They suffer from an excess of word or inaccurate. Uncertainly messages also contributes to their vagueness. Unnecessary repetitions and irrelevant matters in the expression can lead to in barriers in the communication.

(ii) More often negligence of partners is predominant when messages has to be re-routed. Inaccurate translations are the outcome and this becomes a major hurdle in communication. The language that is sometime should be understood by the receiver.

(iii) Sometimes it is very difficult to know that the receiver has understand the same meaning as the sender knows or as per the receiver understands it differently, the purpose is lost. Many words have multiple meanings. The meaning that comes to your mind first depends on your occupation. For example 'charge' may mean electrical charge to an engineering student but fee/rent to a commerce student.

(iv) In transmission process the sentences can convey entirely different meanings depending upon how they are spoken. Consider the sentence "what can I do for you". It means something different with every stage of emphasis from one word to another.

(v) Within the interpretation process words having different meanings. These words are mostly used to refer to inanimate objects.

III. Psychological Barriers

The psychological barriers can be described here:

(i) People have personnel feelings, desires, fears and hopes, likes and dislikes, views, attitude and opinions. Some of these are formed by family background and social environment. They form a sort of emotional filter around the mind and interpret influences on the contents and interpretation of message.

(ii) The 'personal viewpoints', Intellectual background, attributes, understanding, interpretations, some learning attitudes and narrow mindedness also limits the ability to adopt new ideas.

(iii) Sometimes we pay attention to the messages which are useful and often do not pay enough attention to those uninterested messages. The self interest and self-centered attitudes may prevent us from attention for others.

(iv) When we aren't able to understand the language or any other symbols used in the messages, due to inappropriate or unfavorable level of intelligence.

(v) Sometimes many of our ideas, feelings, attitudes and values are influenced and picked up from our social circle or a group. We remain loyal with our group to which we belongs or a particular class of society. We tend to reject an idea which goes against the interest of the group and it becomes a barrier to communication.

(vi) Self image is our idea about what we are, what we look like and what impression we make. It is usually based on some truth and exaggeration of our good points. Due to differences in self images and feelings, the mental and communicative feedback may differ.

(vii) If a person feels threatened by a message he become defensive and responds in such ways that reduce understanding. Such defensive behaviour develops particularly some harmful barrier in handling complaints, grievances and in resolving conflicts.

(viii) A superior person who is conscious of status finds it difficult to receive any suggestions from subordinates. People in senior positions often develop the feeling that they know everything about business. They don't develop their affectionate feelings within their communication with subordinates.

(ix) Some people strongly avoid or resist new ideas which are against their established opinions or traditions. They feel insecure or afraid of change and do not accept a new concept that goes against their cherished ideas. It makes the communication barrier.

(x) When any communication is repeated more than the required number of times, it tends to become a hindrance.

IV. Organizational Barriers

Organizational barriers are also an important part within the study of communication barriers. Organizational barriers arise due to defects in organizational structure, centralization, decentralization, equalities, authoritarian system etc. Sometime; we include the organizational change and reforming efforts for developing the innovative measures. The problems or obstacles as given here are being creating the barriers in communication.

(i) Lack of adequate knowledge and skill of people;

(ii) Lack of availability of proper, adequate and complete information about work performance;

(iii) There is lot of time consuming process of managerial control;

(iv) There is negligent behaviour of the higher authorities and managerial cadres;

(v) There is much emphasizes on formal way of communication as well as formal organizational structure;

(vi) There is not ascertaintity of rights and responsibilities of employees in the organization.

(vii) There is lack of group behaviour, group decision, liasioning and self coordination etc.

(viii) When the scalar chain is unduly long and the distance between top managers and workers increases it becomes delay and distortions in the transmission process.

V. Cross Cultural Barriers

Culture is conceptually shared set of ideas, values, conceptions and attributes of person or a group of persons. It is so much a part of an individual's manner of talking, attributes and behaviour. The globalized business environment and differences in socioeconomic scenario, certain significant and most differences are found due to different opinions, concepts, languages, thinking process, social backgrounds, living styles, values, norms of behaviour, social class, relationship, appearances and perceptions etc.

As such cross cultural factors increases the differences among various concepts, values, outlooks, ideas, expected behaviour and relationship etc.

Even in the best of conditions or ecofriendly relations, communication can be very difficult among different persons or unit as they belongs to different culture.

EFFECTS OF COMMUNICATION BARRIERS IN BUSINESS

The effects of communication barriers on different business areas are as given here:

(i) They create doubts and misunderstanding among the persons;

(ii) The barriers are discouraging the informal way of relations;

(iii) They declined the trust, confidence and belongingness in the organization;

(iv) They developed the conflicts and negligencies among employees;

(v) There are poor and defective implementation of the plan and programmes;

(vi) They develop poor coordination and cooperation among people;

(vii) They create the hurdles for making new and changing avenues in management.

In order to develop mutual cooperation and better behaviour the communication barriers must be removed through some amicable and responsive way. The concept and needful view points can be applicable to make fruitful and effective communication.

Questions

(a) Short Questions

(i) What is meant by Communication barriers?

(ii) Give any two Physical barriers.

(iii) What is Semantic barriers?

(iv) Give any two Psychological barriers.

(v) Define cross cultural barriers.

(vi) Briefly state the 'Distance' and 'Physical Noise' as physical barriers.

(b) Descriptive Questions

(i) Define communication barriers. Also state different physical barriers.

(ii) Describe different types of communication barriers in the field of business and management.

●●●

17 Chapter

Effectiveness of Communication

Communication is the pivot point of business and entire structure move around it. It is an important and decisional aspect for the functioning of business and its allied areas. It has the purpose to establish the process of exchange of information and develop proper interactions among people.

In any organization, the effective communication ensures to develop proper line of authority, determine the responsibilities and accountabilities. It is deliberately and consciously establish the amicable means and ways of communication through some norms and directions for better way of communication.

The effectiveness of a communication system measures and evaluate in terms of its objectives achievement, proper transforming messages, developing informal and formal relations, establishing integration and credibility etc.

OBJECTIVES FOR MAKING COMMUNICATION EFFECTIVE

For making better communication the object for it are given here:

(i) To develop the trust, confidence and reliabilities among people;

(ii) To develop positively inner feeling and willingness of people for sharing with data and informations within the transforming process;

(iii) To develop informal as well as personal relations among people;

(iv) To make clear, complete, precise and correct informations to the concerning people;

(v) To develop proper coordination and integration in organization;

(vi) To develop congenial work environment in organization;

(vii) To make effective listeners within the communication process.

Principles of Communication

or

Essentials of Effective Communication

Communication is needful aspect and without it, the business cannot exist. Therefore the businessmen and managers must ensure that the communication system and process is effective. The effective communication system is one which achieves its objectives. Therefore, the essentialities for making communication effective, some of the ideal and directionals concepts and viewpoints may be considered as principles of communication. The principles which provide some worthwhile viewpoints are given here:

(i) Principle of Clarity

This is basic principle that communication should be in simple, easy and commonly understood language. A sender of message makes it meaningful and clearly express its contents that are needful. Therefore the receiver can easily understood and interprets it. As such the transformation of message must be in clear words.

(ii) Principle of Adequacy

Communication should be adequate and complete, not broken or incomplete. Adequacy of message in all respect may save the time and develop the effective relations and understanding among partners.

(iii) Principle of Informality

The view points and procedural framework must be develop some informal relations particularly between higher executives and subordinates. Some time the informality among messages and in its transmission must be followed for making effective communication.

(iv) Principle of Time

All the messages and informations should be communicated at the proper time. The process of communication should not only ensure that the message reaches the receiver when he actually required. The time factor is an important and decisional part for effective communication.

(v) Principle of Consistency

The contents and basic objectives of messages should be consistent with the missions, plans, programmes of the enterprise. It must include the entire content which is more relevant with the aims and objectives of communication. Better planning and other managerial functions can be achieved by consistent communication.

(vi) Principle of Attention

The attention of receiver on the communicated message must be drawn to make the communication effective. The recipients' attention is very needful which depends upon the contents and effectiveness of the message.

(vii) Principle of Integrity

Communication is a means to develop proper cooperation and coordination to make that work accomplished satisfactory. It is the policy of integration to develop mutual efforts, trust and confidence for better communication.

(viii) Principle of Empathy

In the system of communication, the socio-psychological factors must be considered. The sender must consider the feelings, emotions, viewpoints and perceptions of the receiver. The most important spirit of cooperation is to make empathy in communication.

(ix) Principle of Credibility

The foremost principle of the communication is that it has credibility or believability. The message or fact or informations should be trustworthy and develop some credibility of the concerns.

(x) Principle of Effective Listening

To communicate effectively, one should be good listener. The senders in particular should develop the habit, conscious, inner feelings, cooperative attitude, positive thinking and patient for better listening from the another partners.

(xi) Principle of Feedback

Communication is not complete unless the response or reaction of the receiver of the message is obtained by the communicator. The feedback is very important part from the receiver for encouragement and needful modifications in the communication.

(xii) Principle of Participation

Sometimes, the sender can invite the receiver an any recipient in the process of preparation and determining the contents of message. This is helpful for making proper trust and understanding the objectives of message.

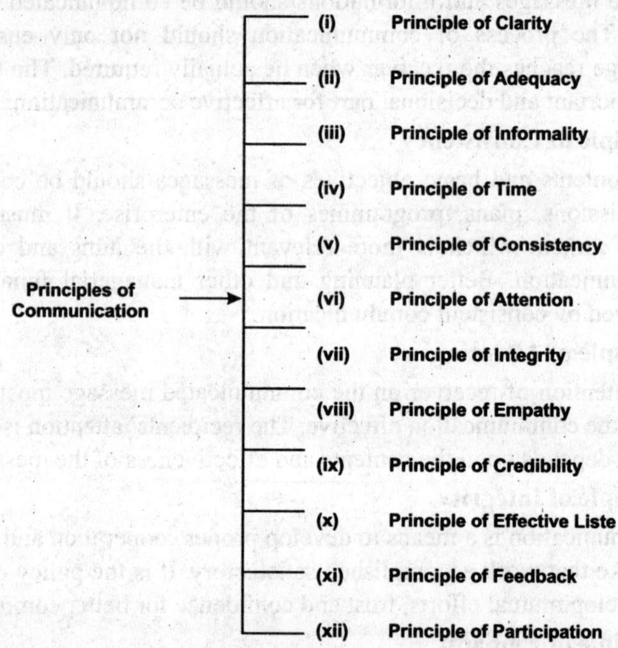

Table 16: Showing the Suggestive Means within Applicability of the Types/Forms of Communication for Making its Effectiveness

Here, the suggestive measures or aspects towards the applicability of various types or forms of communication are given here:

Types or Forms of Communication	Suggestive Means for Making Effective Communication
I. On the basis of Direction/Flow (i) Downward (ii) Upward	- Proper attention - Participation - Suggestive communication
II. On the basis of Scope/Area (i) Internal (ii) External	- Conciseness - Credibility - Completeness
III. On the basis of Organizational Structure (i) Formal (ii) Informal	- Effective listening - Informality - Empathy
IV. On the basis of Organization Status (i) Individual based (ii) Group based	- Express accountabilities - Avoid duplication of message - Comprehensive informations
V. On the basis of Media (i) Oral (ii) Written (iii) Gestural (iv) Visual aids	- Clarity - Appropriate body language - Proper visual media
VI. On the basis of Nature (i) Informative (ii) Inter personal (iii) Organizational	- Completeness - Integration - Follow the hierarchy level

The suggestive measures as given here, might be applicable towards different forms, types and means of communication within their working performance. Basically, these forms & means of communication can be divided into six major parts. The suggestive aspects formulate the perspective areas for effective communication. These aspects can be able to remove the communication barriers related to different forms or means of communications. As such, it is needful for making a better and appropriate applicability of the different types or forms of communication through these suggestive aspects.

THE 7'C FOR GOOD/OPTIMUM/EFFECTIVE COMMUNICATION

In order to make an appropriate and effective communication, there is a need to develop proper system and techniques. Here, some of the basic aspects depends upon some principles and guidelines are studied here as 7C. These are the appropriate and optimum means to make communication effective.

I. Clarity

The concept of clarity implies both clarity of views, concepts and thoughts as well as clarity of expressions. Clarity of thought express that the communicator must be fully determined about what he wants to communicate (the message), why he wants to communicate, to whom he wants to communicate etc. As such clarity of expressions required to avoid all ambiguities, words of double messages and non familiar messages. It is required to use simple words, verbal and non verbal symbols with simple language.

II. Consideration

In order to communicate effectively, several considerable aspects should be adopted by sender and informers. In fact they, as the first person, should think and prepare a mental preparedness and look from the receiver's angle. The human aspects, emotions, sentiments and socio-psychological factors of the receiver must be considered and understood.

III. Completeness

Every communication must be complete and adequate. Every person or any unit as sender should be provided with all the needful facts, figures and informations. In order to ensure completeness of message, the partners should clarify all the queries or any questions as raised within the contents of message.

IV. Correctness

The sender or any person should be absolutely assured with the accuracy, correctness and authenticity of informations. The transmission of any false or incorrect message may develop misunderstanding and spoil the mutual relations. Delayed and outdated messages must be discouraged. So correctness in all respect is necessary.

V. Conciseness

The contents of message must be in fewest possible words. It is needful to adopt the concept of brevity which is the soul of good and appropriate communication. It provides to save time and grace of speech to and prepare an optimum size of message.

VI. Courtesy

Within the process and purview of communication, the amicable, friendly and helpful behaviour are needful to make the desired message fruitful. The examples are as apologize for an omission, avoid irritating expressions, true and fair contents, promptly reply, use empathy and if you have committed a mistake then express your regrets promptly and sincerely.

VII. Continuation

The transmitting process should be continue and regular at every stage. Every message must have a nature of continuation. So that the relations can be developed without any interruptions.

Model – 15

The 7'C FOR GOOD/EFFECTIVE COMMUNICATION

Different prominent viewpoints and principles provide some foremost aspects denotes by 7C' are given here.

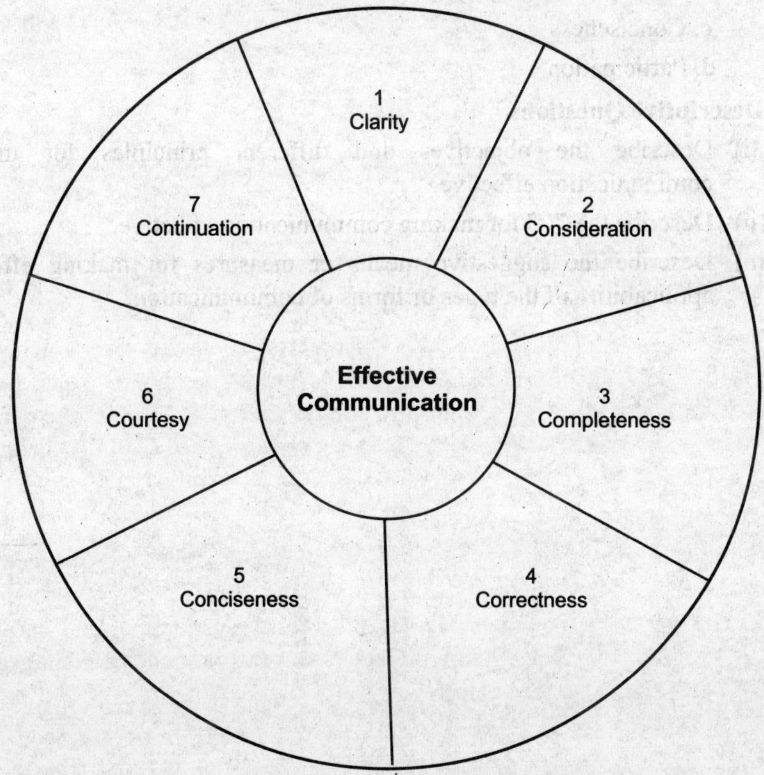

Questions

(a) Short Questions

(i) Give two objectives for making communication effective.

(ii) Give any two main principles for making effective communication.

(iii) Give the suggestive measures for making communication effective on the basis of area or scope.

(iv) How you give suggestive means for making effective communication on the basis of organisational status & on the basis of media.

(v) Define the following

a. Principles of Time

b. Principle of Integrity

c. Conciseness

d. Participation

(b) Descriptive Questions

(i) Describe the objectives and different principles for making communication effective.

(ii) Describe the 7'C for making communication effective.

(iii) Describe the suggestive means or measures for making effective applicability of the types or forms of communication.

●●●

Glossary

Electronic Cash = Cash transaction by e-mail
Electronic Data Interchange = Data transforming process
Electronic Payment = Payment by electronic mail
Electronic Mail = Net mail
Enterprise Resource Planning = Planning for resource allotments
Credit Card = A payment instrument used in internet
Facsimile = Manuscript
File Transfer Protocol = FTP
Formal = Conventional
Feed Back = Response
Synonyms = Similar words
Antonyms = Opposite words
Archival = Records
Abstract = Specific object – Short form
Appearance = Present
Abrupt = Sudden
Computer Aided Design = CAD
Server = Data provides to many client PC's
Dial-up Modem = Most popular intermittent connection
Clients PC = A part or body of computer to maintain informations
DSL Connection = A high bandwidth digital connection
Diskettes = Floppy dish
Dumbest = Stupid
Documentation = Evident
Downward = Top to bottom

Internet = Global views

Imbibe = Absorb the inner feeling

Integrated = Combining

Interprete = Explicate

Informal = Casual

I.S.D.N. = Int. Serv. Digital Network

Body Language = Facial expression non verbal gestures

Voice Mail = Verbal mailing

Grapevine = A usually unrevealed source of confidential information

Horizontal = Parallel

Logical = Valid

Listening = Communicating

Conversation = Informal interchange

Multidimensal = Wide aspects

Memo = Note to remember

Minutes = Moment (small amount of time)

Media = Communication

Multi Media = Different media

Modularity = Resembling

Predictability = Forecasting

Network = Many lines crossing each other

Redundancy = Overlapping

Listening = Communicating

Web Browser = A program that gives a computer instructions that provide the user with tools to accomplish a task; "he has tried several different word processing applications".

Websites = A group of connected pages on the World Wide Web containing information on a particular subject.

Web page = The opening page of a web site.

Transmitting = Passing

Teleconferencing = A discussion among participants who have an agreed (serious) topic.

World Wide Web (WWW) = A popular service to provide internet servers.

Pause = Stop, rest

Prone = Tending recumbent

Pie Charts = Graphic representation

Pictograms = Object

Software = The programs, routines, and symbolic languages that control the functioning of the hardware and direct its operation.

Signals = Indication

Salutation = Gestures

Semantic = Of or related to meaning, especially meaning in language.

Symbols = Emblem, sign

Sender = Transmitter

Systems = Method

●●●

References

- Akhter S.N. – "Computer Fundamentals", Shree Niwas Publications, Jaipur
- Bansal Ram – "Information System : Analysis and Design". 2004
- Bharihoke, Deepak – "Fundamentals of Information Technology", Excell Books, New Delhi
- Chunawala S.A. – "Mass Communication and Media Studies", Himalaya Publishing House, Mumbai
- D.S. Yadav – "Foundation of Information Technology", 2008
- De Cesare – "Development of Component based Information System"
- Debashish and Das – "Business Communication" , PHI Publications"
- Dubey – "I.T. Strategy and Management"
- Goyal, Ritendra – "Computer Applications in Management"
- Goyal, Ritendra – "E–Commerce"
- Jain V.K. – "Information Technology", Excell Books, New Delhi
- Jerone Kanter – "Management – Oriented – MIS"
- Joseph – "E–Commerce : An Indian Perspective", PHI Publications
- Joshi N.K. Shrivastava – "Information Technology for Management"
- Joyce and Moon – "Microsoft Office System", PHI Publications
- Kapoor V.K. – "Quantitative Techniques, System Analysis and Data Processing"
- Karan Sareen – "Business Communication"
- Khanna, Rajive – "Computer Application" (Hindi)
- Manisha Chopra – "Office Management"
- Martin – "Principles of Data Base Management", PHI Publications
- Mischal, V.P. – "Communication and Research for Management"
- Murthy C.S.V. – "Management Information System", Himalaya Publishing House, New Delhi
- N. Foster – "Dictionary of Grammer and Styles"
- Namita Gopal – "Business Communication"